FORCED
INTO FAITH

FORCED
INTO FAITH
HOW RELIGION ABUSES CHILDREN'S RIGHTS

INNAIAH NARISETTI

FOREWORD BY NAVEENA HEMANTH

Prometheus Books

59 John Glenn Drive
Amherst, New York 14228-2119

Published 2009 by Prometheus Books

Inquiries should be addressed to
Prometheus Books
59 John Glenn Drive
Amherst, New York 14228–2119
VOICE: 716–691–0133, ext. 210
FAX: 716–691–0137
WWW.PROMETHEUSBOOKS.COM

13 12 11 10 09   5 4 3 2 1

Library of Congress Cataloging-in-Publication Data

Innaiah, Narisetti, 1937–
    Forced into faith : how religion abuses children's rights / by Innaiah Narisetti.
        p. cm.
    Includes bibliographical references.
    ISBN 978–1–59102–606–8
    1. Religious education of children. 2. Child abuse—Religious aspects. 3. Religion—Controversial literature. 4. Convention on the Rights of the Child (1989). I. Title.
BL42.I56 2008
200.83—dc22

2007051810

Printed in the United States on acid-free paper

*To my son
Raju Narisetti*

CONTENTS

FOREWORD
by Naveena Hemanth

Do children have religions? The simple answer is no, children do not have religions. That is, they are not born with religions; they are born into the religions of their families.

A religion is a system of belief and a way of life dictated by that system of belief that a child is forced to adopt without understanding the implications behind it. We therefore do not have a Hindu, Christian, Muslim, or Buddhist child; we have a child from a Hindu, Christian, Muslim, or Buddhist family.

How are children indoctrinated? Parents and grandparents, extended family members, and caregivers preach morals and religious tenets through the telling of religious stories. Hindus tell children about karma, or the expectation of rebirth/reincarnation based on sins or good deeds done in this lifetime. Similarly, Muslims tell children about heaven and hell. Christians talk about a loving God who will return to Earth and take everyone who has followed in his ways to heaven, or condemn unbelievers to hell if they have strayed. Like members of other religions, they also talk about figures such as Satan and angels as well as concepts of sin and atonement. Every religion has rules to live by. Their common theme is: *Do all that you are told and you will be God's child and get to heaven; do not follow these rules and you are sure to be evil and will go to hell.*

So what happens to children when such religious beliefs and superstitions are inculcated at a young age? This is the critical question that needs to be answered.

In the field of child development, temperament, and psychology, we have substantial research literature that directly links parenting styles to children's adjustment. Infants and children learn by emulating their parents or other caregivers. They recognize facial expressions and voice intonations very early on. They want to please their parents and innately want to do well and be good, as well as to learn, have much curiosity, socialize, feel, and emote. Channeling these aspects of normal growth and development should be the primary goal of parents and communities at large. When such development is injected with fear of the unknown, evil entities, and severe punishment for questioning beliefs or displaying critical thinking, the innate human capacity for appropriate decision making may be affected.

We place certain age restrictions on drug and alcohol consumption, driving, voting, marriage, employment, medical treatments, and so on. In the area of education, much research has been done with regard to what subjects can be effectively and appropriately taught to children of various backgrounds; that is, what a child of a given age is ready to learn. (For example, sex education is not taught to kindergarteners.) Similarly, religious education may need regulations based on age appropriateness and child development.

I must thank my older son, Josh, for asking a question that really got me thinking. He was about five years old when he came home one day and asked, "Mom, if Christians say all non-Christians will go to hell, and Muslims say all non-Muslims will go to hell, then will we all go to hell? Or are there different hells for different people?"

What a question! I do not know the answer. *Do you?*

PREFACE

RELIGION AND CHILD ABUSE: AN UNACKNOWLEDGED GLOBAL PHENOMENON

O ver the years, the abuse of children has received a lot of attention worldwide. The United Nations, through its member organizations such as the United Nations Educational, Scientific, and Cultural Organization (UNESCO), has focused on this issue, recognizing the worst forms of such abuse, including child labor. An estimated 250 million children are engaged in some form of work due to the practice of slavery, bondage linked to family debts, or serfdom, as well as forced recruitment and involvement in armed conflicts, child pornography and prostitution, and the production and trafficking of illicit drugs.

The International Labor Organization, the United Nations Children's Fund (UNICEF), and UNESCO hold regular discussions at various levels, organize international conventions, and have adopted a world declaration for protection of children.

The Convention on the Rights of the Child

The human rights of children and the standards to which all governments must aspire in realizing these rights for all children are most concisely and fully articulated in one international human rights treaty: the Convention on the Rights of the Child. The convention is the most universally accepted human rights instrument in history. It has been ratified by every country in the world, except two: the United States and Somalia. It places children at center stage in the quest for the universal application of human rights. By ratifying this convention, national governments have committed themselves to protecting and ensuring children's rights and have agreed to hold themselves accountable for this commitment before the international community.

While it is unfortunate that a powerful country such as the United States has yet to ratify the Convention on the Rights of the Child, UN efforts are salutary and place much needed emphasis on improving the lives of children globally.

The Influence of Religion

Despite all the effort and rhetoric about protecting children and their rights, however, there is one big gap and a severe shortcoming in the global campaign to protect children: the influence of religion and its continuing contribution to many forms of child abuse all around the world.

Such abuse begins with the involuntary involvement of children in religious practices from the time they are born. All religions, through daily rituals, preaching, and religious texts, seek to bring children into day-to-day religious practice. This gives holy books and scriptures, as well as those who teach them, an early grip on the developing minds of young people, leaving an indelible impression on them. In many cases, most notably in the Catholic Church, this forced and prolonged exposure of children to religious institutions has also been a key factor in the physical and mental abuse of children by religious leaders.

This early grip is so strong that very few people, once grown, ever get an opportunity to change their minds, despite being exposed to science and rational thinking, or even other religious systems. Religious beliefs thrive by inculcating on impressionable minds a blind adherence to certain dogmatic practices. In some ways, this lays the groundwork for sustained psychological abuse of young children by allowing adults the use of religion as a pretext for various other forms of abuse,

such as forcing them to fight in wars in the name of religion and eth-
nicity. During 2004, about three hundred thousand children served as
soldiers in national armies.

When it comes to the forced inculcation of religion and the
resulting abuses of children in the name of religion, the United
Nations, all of its affiliated organizations, and almost all national governments remain steadfastly silent.

The United Nations' Reluctance

In one form or another, all religions violate the rights of children. Yet
an organization like the United Nations, which allows the Vatican to
be represented among its member countries, is unaware of, or more
likely, unable and unwilling to stand up to the religious abuse of children. There is significant pressure from the Vatican to pull back on or
dilute any resolutions that point to religion as a cause of abuse or
strife. Add to this the unwillingness of the United Nations to confront
its member countries, especially those in the Muslim world, which can
also exert a lot of pressure when it comes to issues related to the abuse
of children by religious schools, or *madrassas* (religious schools to
preach faith). For example, very young children are forced to memorize six thousand verses of the Koran, a process that involves both
mental and physical abuse.

As a result, the United Nations and its affiliated agencies tend to
focus on addressing the symptoms rather than the root causes of these
insidious forms of child abuse. For example, while many speak out
against genital mutilation, UNICEF is unwilling to acknowledge and
condemn it because it is considered by some to be a religious practice.
Instead, UNICEF members talk about educating communities and the
organization spends millions of dollars on medical kits to treat children who have already been mutilated. By not forcefully pointing the
finger at the real culprit—religious practices—UNICEF is not only
missing a good opportunity to stem the problem at its source but is
also putting a bandage on a much deeper malaise.

Gender Discrimination

Another area in which religions contribute to child abuse is through implicit and explicit gender discrimination that leads to unequal rights status between boys and girls and contributes to further abuses, especially as it relates to a lack of equal opportunity for females. While economic factors are also to blame, the roots of this inequity lie in religious and social mores. How can the United Nations hope to tackle the problem of child labor or a lack of educational opportunity among the 130 million children in developing countries who are not in primary school, the majority of them being girls? In the Islamic world, some female students are allowed to attend certain madrassas. However, they are forced to learn in separate classrooms or buildings, away from males.

There is a global unwillingness to acknowledge that all religions use educational institutions and programs, be they Sunday schools, madrassas, or Jewish or Hindu temples and their respective programs to indoctrinate children. Sometimes this is in the guise of conveying good moral values, but while it may be much more rigid and overt in, say, a madrassa, it is no less influential on young minds in a Sunday school.

Ultimately, all such programs try to instill a belief in the superiority of one religion and inculcate an unquestioning faith in that system.

Conclusion

Just as most stand up against child marriage because marriage is an institution meant for adults, and just as most do not let children participate in certain civic duties such as voting until they reach a certain age, the time has come to debate the participation of children in religious institutions. While some might see it as a matter best left to parents, the negative influence of religion and its subsequent contribution to child abuse from religious beliefs and practices begs the question of whether organized religion is an institution that needs limits set on how early it should have access to children.

There is no doubt that this will be a controversial position. However, there is nothing to prevent the United Nations from organizing a world convention on the issue of the religious abuse of children, a forum where the pros and cons of childhood exposure to religion and its influence on children can be openly debated. The United Nations cannot remain silent on this vital issue just because it is a sensitive and difficult subject, even given its member nations and their religious interests. A discussion like this would also be an opportunity for those who might want to argue *for* the benefits of the influence of religion on children, so the United Nations should not shy away from debating the issue.

If such a convention clearly shows that religion contributes to child abuse globally, the United Nations must then take a clear stand on the issue of the forced involvement of children in religious practices; it must speak up for the rights of children and not the automatic right of parents and societies to pass on religious beliefs.

Until this happens, millions of children worldwide will continue to be abused in the name of religion, and the efforts made by the United Nations will continue to address only the symptoms but not the disease.

ACKNOWLEDGMENTS

I am thankful to Baror International, Inc. for allowing to quote from *God Is Not Great* of Christopher Hitchens; to women unlimited for permitting me to quote from *My Girlhood* of Taslima Nasrih; and Simon & Schuster for permitting me to quote from *Infidel* of Ayaan Hirsi Ali.

PART I

INTRODUCTION

Our children are our own.
They are ours to thrash or kill, if we choose.
Who are you to poke your nose in?

Millions of parents still feel that way, in every part of the world. They justify harsh punishments with dictums like "you can train a plant but not a tree" or "spare the rod and spoil the child." Too many traditional religions encourage parents to regard children as their property—or to believe that the more children they have, the better: "A child has not only a mouth but also two earning hands." Where do sayings like these come from? Which social institutions underlie much of the child abuse endemic to world today, yet are scarcely ever accused by name? Religions, of course. It is religions that inspire and perpetuate much of the abuse that afflicts children around the globe.

Over the ages, religions have exploited the power of the bond between parents and children, fashioning priestly infrastructures that touch every aspect of life, enmeshing families ever deeper in allegiance. In most cultures this entrapment begins at or soon after birth with the naming of the baby. Parents feel it is their duty to abide by religious customs, traditions, and rituals. This, in turn, assures a continued livelihood for the priestly class.

Priests encourage parents to bring their children along when they visit places of worship. Parents obey, often hoping that experiences in the temple, church, mosque, or synagogue and Buddhist centers will help children develop faith in God and practice ethical conduct. Children are thus controlled right from birth, in all countries and in all religions. Believing parents do not merely indoctrinate their children on the virtues of their own religions, they also warn their young against embracing other religions and following their customs and beliefs.

WHAT IS ABUSE?

Belief may be permanent if the information entering the thalamus coincides with a high state of emotional arousal, such as fear or the thrill of victory. The chemical messengers of emotion cause the thalamus to bypass the sensory cortex and route the information directly to the amygdale. This is often the origin of what might be called personal superstitions—the cricketer who won't play without his lucky hat, for example. People develop elaborate rituals in an effort to re-create the conditions that surrounded some rewarding experience or to avoid conditions their brains associate with fear or pain. People often find themselves almost compelled to go through these rituals, even when the cerebral cortex is telling them that a causal connection is highly implausible.

This kind of belief generation was going on long before our ancestors began to resemble humans, of course, but the advent of language opened a powerful new channel, both for the formation of beliefs and for their reinforcement. Speech exposes persons to the generation of shared beliefs—beliefs based not on personal experience but on experiences related by others. This has the potential to spare a lot of unpleasantness. For example, everyone need not discover the hard way that a particular plant is poisonous. The shared beliefs of a family or tribe are also a powerful force of social cohesion and are reinforced throughout their lives. Language makes vicarious experience the dominant source of belief in humans, overwhelming personal experience. The power of language was enormously amplified by the invention of writing and continues to be amplified by every new advance in communication, from the printing press to the World Wide Web. Beliefs can now spread around the world in the twinkling of a computer chip. That which allows people to learn from others, unfortunately, also exposes them to manipulation by persons.

Small children are particularly open to new beliefs, accepting without question whatever they are told by adults. Their belief engine runs freely, finding few previous beliefs to contradict what they are told. For a small child who must quickly learn that stoves burn and strange dogs bite, this sort of credulity is important to survival, because childrens' beliefs are not enmeshed in a network of related beliefs; however, children seem able to cast them off almost as early as they adopt them. Fantastic stories about Santa Claus and Ganesh, the elephant God in India, which are accepted uncritically, are dropped just as uncritically when someone, often a playmate, explains that it isn't really so. Nor do children appear to develop doubts about other things they've been taught just because the truth of the Santa Claus story is revealed.

As the store of beliefs grows, conflicts with existing beliefs become more likely, and doubt begins to manifest itself. By the time the child reaches adolescence, beliefs tend to be enmeshed in an insulating matrix of related beliefs. The belief process becomes decidedly asymmetric: the belief engine is generating beliefs far more easily than it erases them. Once people become convinced that a rain dance produces rain, they do not lose their belief during the years through which the drought persists. They are more likely to conclude that they have fallen out of favor with the elephant god and perhaps add a human sacrifice to the ritual.

The result is that most of us wind up with beliefs that closely resemble those of our parents and community. Society, in fact, often holds it to be a virtue to adhere to certain beliefs in spite of evidence to the contrary. Belief in that which reason denies is associated with steadfastness and courage, while skepticism is often identified with cynicism and weak character. The more persuasive the evidence against a belief, the more virtuous it is deemed to persist in keeping it. Faith can be a positive force, enabling people to persevere in the face of daunting odds, but the line between perseverance and fanaticism is perilously thin. Carried to extremes, faith becomes destructive—take the residents of Jonestown, for example, or the Heaven's Gate cult. In both cases, the faith of the believers was tested; in both cases, they passed the test.

Along with hundreds of adults, 260 children died in a mass suicide after consuming soft drink laced with cyanide in November 1978. American lay minister Jim Jones, who worked in Jonestown in the Guyana jungles since 1977, organized this suicide under the influence of religion. His cult was known as People's Temple. He was an absolute religious leader who believed in his power and his immortality. He tortured children and maimed and murdered anyone who expressed a dissenting voice. He punished children for even minor offenses while their mothers watched helplessly. The cult believed Jim Jones was their god. They practiced idiosyncratic language, isolated themselves, and excluded outsiders. They led a sealed lifestyle. They sought spiritual fulfillment through their cult. Cults have strange belief systems with peculiar religious ideology.

Another famous cult that was developed in the United States was the Branch Davidians, whose followers were under the leadership of David Koresh. He was called Yahweh Koresh. He built a community around the Apocalypse Ranch in Waco, Texas, in 1993. David once was a Seventh Day Adventist. He was obsessed with sex. David raped, tortured, and maimed his own cult followers. In April 1993, eighty-five people died under his leadership after a standoff with the US government.

The primitive machinery of the belief engine is still in place, but evolution didn't stop there. It provided us with an antidote.[1]

Thus are the seeds of hatred sown, directly or indirectly, in impressionable minds.

Children are not born into religion; of necessity, they are born not even knowing what religion is, yet the religion of their parents is passed down to them. By the time a child starts talking she can name her religion because it has been named for her.

Yet parents who are in a particular political party don't attribute it to their kids.

Thus steeped in religion from childhood, most people find they cannot climb free of religion later in life. Many find it impossible to shed this ingrained religious influence, even if they blossom into scientists or technologists. Education helps them carve out their careers, but they practice religion as they always have. Before you believe in anything, science demands that it be subjected to inquiry, analysis, and proof. If something cannot be proven, it should not be blindly believed. But around the world, the educated exempt religion from the scientific scrutiny they apply to everything else. When religion and science conflict, most people follow religion and give science a pass. Because of this, religion stands revealed as a barrier to human development.

All religions violate human rights and the equality of man and woman. Religions respect only divine values. Of late, Dr. Richard Dawkins through his book *The God Delusion*, Christopher Hitchens through his book *God Is Not Great*, and Sam Harris through his book *End of Faith* have provided ample evidence to show how religion per se is damaging, particularly to children. There is enough material to indicate that religion has damaged people from all angles, held them in steep superstitions, delved into blind belief, and slowly but gradually killed the spirit of inquiry.

They do not apply the scientific temperament acquired in the course of their education to matters of religion.

Beholden to their faiths or mired in tradition, parents have too often stood mute; they are helpless spectators to the religious abuse of children. Examples include denial of necessary healthcare to children, practices by several Christian denominations, and the widespread sexual abuse of children by Roman Catholic and other clergy.

Pope Benedict openly admitted to the sexual abuse of children by

Catholic priests in his 2008 tour of the United States. But the Vatican never wishes to change its religious enforcement of celibacy for priests and nuns, which is the root cause of this form of child abuse. Whenever priests indulge in sexual abuse of minors, the higher religious authorities try to save them by transferring the offending priest to another place. Sometimes they say that they would inquire in their inner religious court to escape public law.

There is demand from some sections of Catholic priests in South America for allowing priests to marry.

Circumcision is a very old religious practice. Later, some started defending it as healthy medical practice. There is enough evidence to prove that religions justified circumcision, which is mentioned in their holy books. Ayaan Hirsi Ali, a muslim woman hailing from Somalia, where virtually every girl is circumcised, gave her personal as well as social experience about circumcision. She emphatically asserted the Islamic practice of circumcision. The practice is always justified in the name of Islam. The belief is spread that uncircumcised girls will be possessed by devils, fall into vice and perdition, and become whores. Imams never discourage the practice: they say it keeps girls pure.

No one can describe the fear induced in children by the thought of being subjected to a ritual surgical procedure, a horrendous physical abuse in the name of religious purification, better than someone who has experienced it. Ayaan was subjected to genital mutilation, apparently under unhygienic conditions at the tender age of five. Furthermore, she observed the ritual operation inflicted on her six-year-old sister Mahad and her four-year-old sister Haweya. Ayaan was born to a Western-educated Somali Muslim with modern views of religion. Ayaan's father was a political activist and member of the Somali Salvation Democratic Front. This irked some politicians in power and he was often subjected to government harassment. He was arrested and imprisoned by his government when Ayaan was five years old. Probably by mere coincidence their mother was also away from home.

Ayaan and her sisters were then under the care of their grandmother, an elderly lady who believed in the literal interpretation of

Quran and Hadith. This old lady who observed the traditional Islamic rituals with religious fervor, considered genital mutilation of young girls as something ordained by her God. She obviously believed that not cutting off the clitoris and labia minor from young girls not only brought shame on the family but was also a sin in the eyes of God. This gran mother probably sincerely believed that failure to observe this mandate of the God, Mohammad, and Quran would condemn the entire family to eternal damnation.

Ayaan's father had modern views and he considered genital mutilation a barbaric tradition that should be abolished. That may be the reason Ayaan's older sister who was six years old at that time was not subjected to this abuse. While her father was in jail and mother was away from home, Ayaan had a fight in the religious school which she was then attending. Ayaan writes in her autobiography, *Infidel*, "Not long after that first fight of mine at the Madrassa (religious seminary), Grandma decided that the time was right for us to undergo the necessary and proper dignity of purification."

Ayaan studied in religious schools in Kenya and Saudi Arabia and later in Europe. In Dutch schools she studied social work and obtained a master's degree from the University of Leiden in political science in 2000. These studies opened her mind to true human values. She wrote of her experiences as a five-year-old about the child abuse inflicted on her and her two sisters. "After she made the arrangements, Grandma was cheerful and friendly all week long. A special table was prepared in her bedroom, and various aunts, known and unknown, gathered in the house. When the day itself came I was not frightened, just curious. I had no idea what was going to happen, except that there was a festive atmosphere in the house and all three of us were going to be cleansed."

Ayaan Hirsi Ali (This is her press name so as to disguise her real identity from Islamic extremists who are threatening her life) lived as a good Muslim "by the book and for the book" all through her childhood. In 2002, after realizing the trials and tribulations of Muslim women she renounced her religion and joined an atheist group. Hirsi

Ali wrote the script and provided the voice-over for "Submission," a film produced by Theo Van Gogh, which criticized the treatment of women in Islamic society. Juxtaposed with passages from the Quran were scenes of scantily clad actresses. After Van Gogh was assassinated, Hirsi Ali was given asylum in the United States. She described the gruesome details of the genital mutilation in her 2007 book as follows: "Mahad was on the floor, with her head and arms on Grandma's lap. Two women were holding down her spread-eagled legs, and a strange man was bending down between them. The room was warm and I could smell a mixture of sweat and frankincense. Grandma was whispering in Mahad's ears, 'Don't cry, don't stain your mother's honor. These women will talk about what they have seen. Grit your teeth.' Mahad wasn't making a sound, but tears rolled down her face as she bit into Grandma's shawl. Her face was clenched and twisted in pain. I couldn't see what the stranger was doing, but I could see blood. This frightened me."

This lady who is in her forties was once elected as a member of the Dutch parliament but had to flee the country for fear of her life because Islamic extremists condemned her with a Fatwa (encouragement for any 'true believer' to kill). Her report of what happened to her younger four-year-old sister, Haweya is truly tragic. "But I do remember Haweya's blood-curdling howls. Though she was the youngest—she was four, I five, Mahad six—Haweya must have struggled much more than Mahad and I did, or perhaps the women were exhausted after fighting us, and slipped, because the man made some bad cuts on Haweya's thighs. She carried the scars of them her whole life." In a later section she wrote, "It took Haweya another week to reach the stage of thread removal, and four women had to hold her down. I was in the room when this happened. I will never forget the panic in her face and voice as she screamed with everything in her and struggled to keep her legs closed. Haweya was never the same afterward. She became ill with a fever for several weeks and lost a lot of weight. She had horrible nightmares, and during the day began stomping off to be alone. My once cheerful, playful little sister changed. Sometimes she just stared vacantly at nothing for hours. We all started wetting our beds after the circumcision. In Mahad's case, it lasted a long time."

All through this ordeal their grandmother was saying "Once this long knit is removed you and your sister will be pure." During the course of this surgical operation while this young girl was crying, her grandmother would console "It's just this once in your life, Ayaan. Be brave, he's almost finished." The tragedy is that the conditions of this surgical procedure were unhygienic. Ayaan remembered that when the sewing of the outer labia was finished, the man cut the thread off with his teeth.

This procedure is considered even today, as Ayaan's grandmother did then, by many as a must for their daughters. From a health or scientific point of view and even when performed under most modern hygienic conditions there appears to be no justification, yet this type of child abuse is unfortunately not uncommon in some orthodox communities.

If the civilized world is sometimes outraged by such abuses, it has nonetheless kept quiet—afraid to confront religion head on. Individuals have dared to criticize religions' child abuse, only to be ignored or ostracized as "atheists."

Fortunately, some light shimmers along this dark horizon.

PROCLAIMING CHILDREN'S RIGHTS

On November 20, 1989, the United Nations General Assembly adopted the Convention on the Rights of the Child, proclaiming elementary rights for children worldwide. One hundred and ninety-one countries have so far adopted it. In many of them, so-called Children's Charters have been established, building key provisions of the UN Convention on the Rights of the Child into local law. Still, the so-called Children's Convention has not been ratified everywhere; Somalia, wrecked by civil war and without a stable government, has not done so. Nor has the United States of America! The obvious reason is the force of Christian religions pressuring the government not to accept the charter, lest their grip over children disappear. We hope the United States will ratify the charter soon.

The Children's Convention covers all children below eighteen years of age, recognizing legal rights whose respect is incumbent upon parents, families, and governments. It forbids discrimination based on color, creed, or gender in safeguarding children's rights. Under the convention, every girl and boy, irrespective of territorial boundaries, would enjoy freedom of expression and the right to access information. Governments are to safeguard children's religious freedom, their freedom of thinking, and their right to mix with others. Child rearing is recognized as the primary responsibility of parents, but governments must extend a helping hand when needed. Children are not to be treated as the personal property of parents, and they are not to be abused.

Obviously the Children's Convention describes the way things should be, not the way they are in most parts of the world. To its credit, the United Nations has recognized that the convention's ideals are often violated. The United Nations Children's Fund (UNICEF) has launched a movement to safeguard children from abuse, but this movement is of limited effectiveness because it has tried to proceed without blaming religion. The influence of religion is strong, even at the United Nations. For example, the Vatican has co-opted UNICEF, convening a recent conference at which religious leaders shed crocodile tears over children's plight but took no substantial action. This conference, held in 2000, wanted to have more grip over children and inculcate religious values to avoid abuse. That is how religions perpetuate the tight grip over early preaching through seminaries.

Child abuse rooted in religion was described in sanitized language as a "cultural crisis."

The child abuse in African tribes also goes to the root of religion. The recent research work of Christopher Hitchens in his *God Is Not Great* provides more examples and evidence to that direction.

WHAT IS TAUGHT IN MADRASSAS? JIHAD

The totalitarian nature of Islam is nowhere more apparent than in the concept of jihad, the holy war, whose ultimate aim is to conquer the entire world and submit it to the one true faith, to the law of Allah. Islam alone has been granted the truth in the eyes of many of its followers—there is no possibility of salvation outside it. It is the sacred duty, an incumbent religious duty established in the Koran and the traditions of all Muslims to bring it to all humanity. Jihad is a divine institution, enjoined specifically for the purpose of advancing Islam. Muslims must strive, fight, and kill in the name of God:

> Kill those who join other gods with God wherever you may find them (IX.5–6)
>
> Those who are believers fight in the cause of God . . . (IV.76)
>
> I will instill terror into the hearts of the Infidels, strike off their heads then, and strike off from them every fingertip. (VIII.12)
>
> Say to the Infidels: If they desist from their unbelief, what is now past shall be forgiven them; but if they return to it, they have already before them the doom of the ancients! Fight then against them till strife be at an end, and the religion be all of it God's. (VIII.39–42)
>
> The believers who stay at home . . . are not equal to those who fight for the cause of God. . . . God has promised all a good reward, but far richer is the recompense of those who fight for Him. (IV.95)
>
> It is a grave sin for a Muslim to shirk the battle against the unbelievers, those who do will roast in hell;
>
> Believers, when you meet the unbelievers preparing for battle do not turn your backs to them. (Anyone who does) shall incur the wrath of God and hell shall be his home; an evil dwelling indeed. (VIII.15,16)
>
> If you do not fight, He will punish you severely, and put others in your place. (IX.39)
>
> Those who die fighting for the only true religion, Islam, will be amply rewarded in the life to come;
>
> Let those fight in the cause of God who barter the life of this world for that which is to come; for whoever fights on God's path,

whether he is killed or triumphs. We will give him a handsome reward. (IV.74)

It is abundantly clear from many of the above verses that the Koran is not talking of metaphorical battles or of moral crusades; it is talking of the battlefield. To read such bloodthirsty injunctions in a holy book is shocking.

Mankind is divided into two groups—Muslims and non-Muslims. Muslims are members of the Islamic community, the Umma, who possess territories of the Dar al-Islam, the Land of Islam, where the edicts of Islam are fully promulgated. The non-Muslims are the Harbi, people of the Dar al-Harb, the Land of warfare, meaning any country belonging to the infidels that has not been subdued by Islam, but that nonetheless, is destined to pass into Islamic jurisdiction either by con- version or by war (Harb). All acts of war are permitted in the Dar al- Harb. Once the Dar al-Harb has been subjugated, the Harbi will become prisoners of war. The Imam can do what he likes to them according to the circumstances.[3]

HOW DOES ISLAM DEFY HUMAN RIGHTS?

Let us look at the Universal Declaration of Human Rights of 1948 and compare it with Islamic law and doctrine.

Article 1: All human beings are born free and equal in dignity and rights. They are endowed with reason and conscience and should act toward one another in a spirit of brotherhood.

Article 2: Everyone is entitled to all rights and freedoms set forth in this declaration, without distinction of any kind, such as race, color, sex, language, religion, political or other opinion, national or social origin, property, birth or other status.

Article 3: Everyone has the right to life, liberty, and security of person.

Article 4 : No one shall be held in slavery or servitude; slavery and the slave trade shall be prohibited in all their forms.

Comments

1. Women are inferior under Islamic law; their testimony in a court of law is worth half that of a man; their movement is strictly restricted; they cannot marry non-Muslims.
2. Non-Muslims living in Muslim countries have inferior status under Islamic law; they may not testify against a Muslim. In Saudi Arabia, following a tradition of Muhammad, who said, "Two religions cannot exist in the country of Arabic," non-Muslims are forbidden to practice their religion, build churches, possess Bibles, etc.
3. Nonbelievers-atheists (surely the most neglected minority in history) do not have "the right to life" in Muslim countries. They are to be killed. Muslim doctors of law generally divide sins into great sins and little sins. Of the seventeen great sins, unbelief is the greatest, more heinous than murder, theft, adultery, etc.
4. Slavery is recognized in the Koran. Muslims are allowed to cohabit with any of their female slaves (sura 4:3); they are allowed to take possession of married women if they are slaves (sura 4:28). The helpless position of the slave in regard to his or her master illustrates the helpless position of the false gods of Arabic in the presence of their Creator (sura 16:77).

Article 5. No one shall be subjected to torture or the cruel, inhuman or degrading treatment or punishment.

Comment

We have seen what punishments are in store for transgressors of the Holy law: amputations, crucifixion, stoning to death, and floggings. I suppose a Muslim could argue that these were not unusual for a Muslim country, but what of their inhumanity? Again, a Muslim could contend that these punishments are of divine origin and must not be judged by human criteria. By human standards, they are inhuman.[4]

CHILD ABUSE BY RELIGIOUS CULTS IN AFRICA

In northern Uganda there is a center for the rehabilitation of kidnapped and enslaved children in the land of the Acholi people, who live on the northern side of the Nile. The listless, vacant, hardened little boys (and some girls) narrated their stories to Christopher Hitchens during his visit in 2005.[5] They were distressed. The children, between ages eight to thirteen, had been seized from their schools or homes by a stone-faced militia that was itself originally made up of abducted children. Marched into the bush, they were "initiated" in one of two ways; They either had to take part in a murder in order to feel "dirtied up" and implicated, or they had to submit to a prolonged and savage whipping, often of up to three hundred strokes. ("Children who have felt cruelty," said one of the elders of the Acholi people, "know very well how to inflict it.") The misery inflicted by this army of wretches was almost beyond computation. They had razed villages, created a vast refugee population, committed hideous crimes such as mutilation and disemboweling, and had continued to kidnap children so that the Acholi were wary of taking strong countermeasures lest they kill or injure one of their "own."

The name of the militia was the Lord's Resistance Army (LRA), and it was led by a man named Joseph Kony, a passionate former altar boy who wanted to subject the area to the rule of the Ten Commandments. He baptized by oil and water, held fierce ceremonies of punishment and purification, and ensured his followers against death. He was a fanatical preacher of Christianity. The rehabilitation center was also run by a fundamentalist Christian organization. Kony's authority arose in part from his background in a priestly Christian family. It was also true that people were apt to believe he could work miracles, by appealing to the spirit world and promising his acolytes that they were death-proof. Even some of those who had run away would still swear that they had seen wonders performed by the man. All that a missionary could do was try and show people a different face of Christianity.

Joseph Kony is obviously far from the Christian "mainstream." For one thing, his paymasters and armorers are the cynical Muslims of the Sudanese regime, who use him to make trouble for the government of Uganda, which has in turn supported rebel groups in Sudan. In an apparent reward for this support, Kony at one stage began denouncing the keeping and eating of pigs, which, unless he has become a fundamentalist Jew in his old age, suggests a payoff to his bosses. These Sudanese murderers, in their turn, have for years been conducting a war of extermination not just against the Christians and animists of southern Sudan, but also against the non-Arab Muslims of the Darfur province. Islam may officially make no distinction between races and nations, but the slaughterers in Darfur are Arab Muslims and their victims are African Muslims. The "Lord's Resistance Army" is nothing but a Christian Khmer Rouge sideshow in this more general horror.

An even more graphic example is demonstrated in the case of Rwanda, which in 1992 gave the world a new synonym for genocide and sadism. This former Belgian possession is the most Christian country in Africa, boasting the highest percentage of churches per head, with 65 percent of Rwandans professing Roman Catholicism and another 15 percent adhering to various Protestant sects. The words "per head" took on a macabre ring in 1992, when at a given signal the racist militias of "Hutu Power," incited by state and church, fell upon their Tutsi neighbors and slaughtered them en masse.

This was no atavistic spasm of bloodletting, but a coldly rehearsed African version of the Final Solution, which had been in preparation for some time. The early warning of it came in 1987 when a Catholic visionary with the deceptively folksy name of Little Pebbles began to boast of hearing voices and seeing visions from the Virgin Mary. The voices and visions were distressingly bloody, predicting massacre and

apocalypse but also—as if in compensation—the return of Jesus
Christ on Easter Sunday 1992. Apparitions of Mary on a hilltop named
Kibeho were investigated by the Catholic Church and announced as
reliable. The wife of the Rwandan president, Agathe Habyarimana,
was especially entranced by these visions and maintained a close rela-
tionship with the bishop of Kigali, Rwanda's capital city. This man,
Monsignor Vincent Nsengiyumva, was also a central committee
member of President Habyarimana's single ruling party, the National
Revolutionary Movement for Development, or the NRMD. This party,
together with other organs of state, was fond of rounding up any
women of whom it disapproved as "prostitutes" and of encouraging
Catholic activists to trash any stores that sold contraceptives. Over
time, the word spread that the prophecy would be fulfilled and that the
"cockroaches"—the Tutsi minority—would soon get what was
coming to them.

When the apocalyptic year of 1994 came and the premeditated and
coordinated massacres began, many frightened Tutsi and dissident
Hutu were unwise enough to try and take refuge in churches. This
made life considerably easier for the government and military death
squads, who knew where to find them and who could rely on priests
and nuns to point out their locations. (This is why so many of the mass
grave sites that have been photographed are on consecrated ground,
and it is also why several clergymen and nuns are in the dock at the
ongoing Rwandan genocide trials.) The notorious Father Wenceslas
Munyeshyaka, a leading figure at the Kigali Cathedral of Saint
Famille, was smuggled out of the country with the assistance of
French priests, but he has since been charged with genocide, with providing lists of civilians to the *interahamwe*, and with the rape of young
refugee women. He is by no means the only cleric to have faced similar charges. Lest it be thought that he was merely a "rogue" priest, we
have the word of another member of the Rwandan hierarchy, the
bishop of Gikongoro, otherwise known as Monsignor Augustin
Misago, being involved.

Bishop Misago was often described as a Hutu power sympathizer;

he had been publicly accused of barring Tutsis from places of refuge, criticizing fellow members of the clergy who helped the "cockroaches," and asking a Vatican emissary who visited Rwanda in June 1994 to tell the pope to "find a place for Tutsi priests because the Rwandan people do not want them anymore." What's more, on May 4, 1994, shortly before the last Marian apparition at Kibeho, the bishop appeared there himself with a team of policemen and told a group of ninety Tutsi schoolchildren who were being held in preparation for slaughter, not to worry because the police would protect them. Three days later, the police helped massacre eighty-two of the children.

Schoolchildren "held in preparation for slaughter." Perhaps you remember the pope's denunciation of this ineffaceable crime, and of the complicity of his church in it? Or perhaps you do not, since no such comment was ever made. Paul Rusesabagina, the hero of Hotel Rwanda, remembers Father Wenceslas Munyeshyaka referring even to his own Tutsi mother as a "cockroach." But this did not prevent him, before his arrest in France, from being allowed by the French church to resume his "pastoral duties." As for Bishop Misago, there were those in the postwar Rwandan Ministry of Justice who felt that he should be charged as well. But, as one of the officials of the ministry phrased it, "The Vatican is too strong, and too unapologetic, for us to go taking on bishops. Haven't you heard of infallibility?"

At a minimum, this makes it impossible to argue that religion causes people to behave in a more kindly or civilized manner.[6]

UN agencies have recognized that children are being used as bonded laborers and are abused in wars, sexually assaulted, and more. These agencies have strived to rescue victims in some places. But they will not identify religion among the principal causes of abuse. Child abuse is impossible to resist when the principal perpetrator cannot—must not—be named. We cannot expect religions to condemn themselves. It is like handing our house keys to a thief with a request to stand guard.

CHILDREN AND RELIGION:
SOME IMMODEST PROPOSALS

Those who escaped from religion have contributed disproportionately to progress and development in all ages. One example is Charles Darwin, the famous nineteenth-century naturalist, and another is the astronomer Carl Sagan.

The urge to learn new things, to study, to conduct research, and to live in tune with nature—all of these things belong to a level above religion. When children are inculcated in religion and compelled to adhere to it, this thwarts brain development.

It is a crime to warn children that they will lose their sight or fall ill if they refuse to worship or raise unpalatable questions. Brains that should blossom with each passing year are instead blunted, and the priests have no objection because a thinking soul is a threat to every religion.

Religion should be taught on scientific lines in schools. Children should learn about all religions, their own and others. They should be taught that gods and demons, devils and apparitions, and heaven and hell are all human creations, and that the world's scriptures are all human works. They should learn that life is supreme and it should be respected. Children should have the freedom to choose any religion or none at all once they reach the age of maturity.

For their part, parents should realize that religion ought not to be ascribed to children as a hereditary trait. Indeed, they should be kept at a distance from religion, just as parents keep them away from politics, obscenity, and pornography.

Again, to quote from Christopher Hitchens on child abuse by religions:

> Sexual innocence, which can be charming in the young if it is not needlessly protracted, is positively corrosive and repulsive in the mature adult. Again, how shall we reckon the harm done by dirty old men and hysterical spinsters, appointed as clerical guardians to

supervise the innocent in orphanages and schools? The Roman Catholic Church in particular is having to answer this question in the most painful of ways, by calculating the monetary value of child abuse in terms of compensation. Billions of dollars have already been awarded, but there is no *price to be out* in the generations of boys and girls who were introduced to sex in the most alarming and disgusting ways by those whom they and their parents trusted. "Child abuse" is really a silly and pathetic euphemism for what has been going on: we are talking about the systematic rape and torture of children, positively aided and abetted by a hierarchy which knowingly moved the grossest offenders to parishes where they would be safer. Given what has come to light in modern cities in recent times, one can only shudder to think what was happening in the centuries where the church was above all criticism. But what did people expect would happen when the vulnerable were controlled by those who, misfits and inverts themselves, were required to affirm hypocritical celibacy? And who were taught to state grimly, as an article of belief, that children were "imps of" or "limbs of" Satan? Sometimes the resulting frustration expressed itself in horrible excesses of corporal punishment, which is bad enough in itself. But when the artificial inhibitions really collapse, as we have seen them do, they result in behaviour which no average masturbating, fornicating sinner could even begin to contemplate without horror. This is not the result of a few delinquents among the shepherds, but an outcome of an ideology which sought to establish clerical control by means of control of the sexual instinct and even of the sexual organs. It belongs, like the rest of religion, to the fearful childhood of our species. Alyosha's answer to Ivan's question about the sacred torture of a child was to say ("softly")—"No, I do not agree." Our reply, to the repellent original offer of the defenseless boy Issac on the pyre, right up to the current abuses and repressions, must be the same, only not delivered so softly.

In accord with ritual, encouraging blind worship and terrorizing children in the name of a deity are no longer acceptable. Parents need to appreciate and accept that children have inherent rights.

In all, 191 countries have signed the Children's Convention, and their parliaments have begun to adopt charters and other legislation to implement it. But it has yet to be adopted by a developed country like the United States. In 1995, the United States formally signed the charter but it has not been approved by the House of Representatives, which is obligatory.

Professor Paul Kurtz, chairman of the Center for Inquiry, is now trying to fight with the government and convince politicians to accept the charter.

Even parents hesitate to support the convention, for fear of losing their grip on their children. Parents may have been brought up entangled in a religious tradition, but they should not impose their rituals, customs, habits, and superstitions on their children as a forced legacy. Now is the time to break with this unhealthy past.

Ultimately, human progress depends on the recognition that implementation of human values will take mankind to higher levels in all spheres. Blind belief and superstition are hindrances to the quest for knowledge and the search for truth.

The very assertion that we live for God is contrary to human values. Children should be rescued from religion; only then can they be restored to humanity.

QUESTIONS AND ANSWERS

What are the recognized forms of child abuse?

Slavery, human trafficking, debt bondage, serfdom, forced labor, armed conflict, prostitution, pornography, illicit activities like drugs, and genital mutilation of girls. These are recognized by the United Nations Educational, Scientific and Cultural Organization (UNESCO) as child abuses to be eliminated.

What is the most neglected right of the child?

Parents should recognize that children are not their property but are human beings with the right to develop independent of religion. Children should be protected from harmful indoctrination so they can develop mental, spiritual, and moral capabilities.

What is the most neglected article in the Charter of the Rights of Children as declared by United Nations?

Article 14 is deliberately neglected and ignored since it touches the right of freedom of religion and practice of religion. The child should be free to choose his religion or not to choose one until he attains the age of eighteen. Till then, the child should be left free from the impositions, the blind beliefs, the abstract thoughts, the unproven concepts, and the superstitions of holy books of all religions. This aspect is not discussed nor propagated while publicizing the charter. The obvious escape is that religious matters are sensitive and touchy. But the damage is done in neglecting this article.

States parties shall respect the right of the child's freedom of thought, conscience, and religion.

States parties shall respect the rights and duties of the parents and, when applicable, legal guardians, to provide direction to the child in the exercise of his or her right in a manner consistent with the evolving capacities of the child.

Freedom to manifest one's religion or beliefs may be subject only to such limitations as are prescribed by law and are necessary to protect public safety, order, health or morals, or the fundamental rights and freedoms of others.

Who is violating these rights of the child?

All religions. UNESCO feels "delicate" or "sensitive" to mention the religious abuses of children. The pope has a seat in United Nations without voting power, which is one of the stumbling blocks to the recognition of the child abuse of religion. Similarly, other religions that participate in conventions on child abuse deliberately avoid mention of religious abuses of children.

What is the main hindrance?

Holy books, religious traditions, customs, superstitions, blind beliefs. Spanking (punishing) children is approved by all religions. The religions apply the principle of "catch them young" and inculcate their blind faith lest the children stray from it. The unrecognized abuses: children forced to memorize holy books, prayers through religious institutions, schools (madrassas of the Muslims), Sunday school instruction, and recruiting children for propagating religious cults. Compulsory practice of religious customs like shaving of the head, wearing a particular dress as per religious sanction, militant exercises, and chanting prayers from childhood without understanding the meaning.

Which religion compels children to do such things?

All religions, through their priests, holy men and women, institutions, mutts, churches, and mosques.

What if children aren't schooled in religion?

Parents are induced to follow religious instructions, otherwise they or their families may face social boycotts and be ostracized in their communities. It sometimes leads to excommunication, as well.

Are children scared with an idea of hell?

All major religions at some stage inculcate the idea of hell into the minds of children (Buddhism is an exception). Muslim mullahs induce fear among the children with their concept of hell according to their holy book, the Koran. This hell is full of freezing, boiling, tongue piercing, and so on. The Christian hell differs according to the denomination. There is the Catholic hell, the Baptist hell, the Methodist hell, the Unitarian hell, the Lutheran hell, and so on. There are horrifying details that can scare for life. Boiling tar, piercing flesh, and so on, are used to punish and torment the souls. Jewish hell is described according to the Old Testament. Hindus describe their hell in detail. Again, Hindu hell differs according to the sects and denominations like Vishnu, Siva, and so on.

What about heaven?

Of course there is also description of heaven with all pleasures including sex, wine, and so on. Each religion has its detailed view of heaven. Children go into the world with all these deep impressions that influence them for life. This is clearly child abuse.

What happens with mental infection?

Whatever the parents tell, the children believe. Parents tell children about witches, hell, heaven, punishments in hell, and they will believe. Sunday schools of Christians and Mmadrassas of Muslims further instruct children with all sorts of beliefs, fears, and threats in the name of morals, and children are poisoned with terrible superstitions. Children will become easy prey to blind belief systems from the damaging information of holy books and religious stories. This is mental infection. Children are subverted by mullahs, nuns, and priests everywhere. This is child abuse. With these mental infections of belief, children become intolerant toward other beliefs and other religions. Muslim jihadists lead the call of intolerance and go to the extent of killing people. Christians call others heathens. Hindus depict others as *mlecchas*, or foreign heathens. Whatever is inimical to their faith is treated with intolerance. Faith often leads to suicide also. People are prepared to die for their faith. Jihad among Muslim extremists is one such thing. Children are recruited, sent off to holy wars, and are prepared to die for the holy cause. Only few can come out of blind religious beliefs and do it safely. Children are recruited for Mass service among Catholics. Incidents of pedophilia are rampant. Parents are often dumb witnesses. The pope and Vatican is not prepared to punish priests who indulge in child abuse and often try to save these guilty priests.

UNESCO should recognize that these are aspects of child abuse. Parents take their children to such religious bodies willingly, thinking that the child will develop character, faith, and morals. Christian institutions recruit children at young age for developing them as clergy members. Buddhists recruit for lamas. Hindus recruit for mutts like Sankaracharyas. Muslims are supposed to take their children to Madrassas for them to memorize compulsorily the six thousand suras of the Koran in Arabic (their holy language).

All children are scientifically oriented. They wonder and question without inhibition. Their questions at a primary level indicate innocence, curiosity, and inquisitiveness. All these aspects should be encouraged by parents and teachers. But when faced with questions that they cannot answer, or feel shy to answer, parents and teachers normally start curbing the child from asking such questions.

How was I born?

Every child asks this question at some point. Parents avoid answering correctly. They tell lies. They bring in supernatural elements. Falsehood starts here. At a secondary level children develop hesitation to ask any and every question. That sort of fear is gradually acquired from the primary level. At primary level the kids believe whatever the parents say and the teachers answer. Unfortunately, both parents and teachers inculcate plenty of beliefs and superstitions at that level. "How was I born?" is a universal question asked by kids. Invariably the answer is given with falsehood. "God is the cause for your birth." That answer is the starting point for lying. It goes against causality. If a kid asks, "How was God born?" the answer would be

"You should not ask such questions," "You will become blind if you question God." Skepticism is killed. Even about nature there are several questions from kids.

Where do the stars come from?

Who created the sky and why is it blue? Parents may not know these answers immediately. So it is also with teachers. They should not misdirect or give wrong answers, but they do. That is the starting point for the seed of superstition among kids.

They can say that they will find out the answer and let the kids know. Belief starts thus: Senses gather information. This information goes to the sensory cortex through the thalamus in the brain. Analysis takes place there. Then it reaches the amygdala in the temporal lobes. The amygdala helps respond to the emotions generated by sensory stimuli. Fear, worry, and other similar emotions are typical examples for this. Belief is not retained if it is received only once. But if beliefs are reinforced continuously, then they become permanent. When fear, thrill, and stimuli in thalamus coincide, then the belief is perpetuated. Customs, rituals, and prayers are repeated and become part of children's fears and emotions, and gradually are converted into belief. Whatever is told at a primary level, the children are open to believing. They accept the authority of parents and teachers. Stories about Santa Claus or the Monkey God may be brushed aside as not true after some stage. Rain is supposed to come naturally. During drought periods, believers pray for rain and perform customary rituals. At that juncture, if rain comes, the belief is strengthened. Such beliefs make a strong impact. Belief leads to fanaticism. All religions thrive on such beliefs. Astrology, horoscopes, and similar other beliefs make a strong impact with continuous belief systems. Children acquire these beliefs from parents and teachers and friends.

Children are naturally gullible and credulous. In the early stages, parents are omnipotent to them. Whatever the parents say, children rarely question or take it for granted. Parents may amuse the kids with the gifts of Santa Claus and tell them a make-believe story of how the gifts are distributed through chimney in the night. At some stage children must be told the truth. Otherwise, the belief perpetuates. Similarly, other stories from the Bible, the Koran, and several holy books must be explained to children as pure fiction. Especially when fearful aspects are told like hell and demons, elders must precede by warning children that what is being told to them are merely entertaining stories.

Do children have rights?

Yes. One hundred and ninety-one countries in 1991 ratified the world declaration of the Convention on the Rights of Child. The United Nations General Assembly unanimously adopted this declaration. Each country has to implement the rights of children after enacting it through the elected bodies. What are the impediments? Religion is the main hindrance. Each religion has its laws, holy books, customs, conventions, and superstitions, which are harmful to children. UNESCO does not mention the religious child abuses because religion is viewed as a delicate field. Female genital mutilation is one typical example where UNESCO did not bring in religion, though the practice is recognized as child abuse.

What are the broad issues of child abuse in religions?

Some assert that children have to be caught while young and taught compliance with religion: "After all, you can train a plant but not a tree." Others swear by the dictum, "Spare the rod and spoil the child."

Most parents regard their children as their property. They believe that the greater the number of children, the better off they are. A child has not only a mouth but also two earning hands.

There are parents who honestly feel that children should follow them in thought, word, and deed and subscribe to and live according to their religious beliefs and customs. For children, parents constitute their universe. A parent's speech is, therefore, sacrosanct and inviolable.

Against this backdrop, children are lured into the trap of religion. Over the ages, a religious dimension has been added to every aspect of life, beginning with the naming of the baby soon after birth. Parents feel it is their duty to abide by religious customs, traditions, and rituals. This, in turn, assures livelihood to the priestly class.

Priests encourage parents to bring along their children to places of worship. Parents fall in line as they think temple visits help children develop faith in God and follow ethical conduct. Children are thus controlled right from their birth in all countries and in all religions.

Children are neither born into religion nor aware of what religion is. Yet, the religion of their parents is attributed to them. By the time they start talking and writing, they name their religion. Thus steeped in religion from childhood, most find it difficult to climb out of it later on in life.

If something cannot be proved, it should not be blindly believed. But the educated exclude religion from such scientific scrutiny. One thus gets mired in religious beliefs. When there is a conflict between religion and science, people often follow religion and pass on science. Religion has thus become an eternal and insurmountable barrier to humankind's progress and development.

This is a Herculean task, to educate parents, teachers, and society in general. But this uphill task should be undertaken by voluntary organizations, United Nations branches, and governments. It will take a long time. Media can play vital role in this field.

The silver lining in the dark horizon is that at long last, the United Nations has become cognizant of religious perversities. It convened a global conference and facilitated the adoption of a Children's Charter.

A CHILDREN'S CHARTER

The charter covers all children below eighteen years of age. There shall be no discrimination based on caste, color, creed, or gender in safeguarding children's rights. Where parents fail to take care of children, the government shall assume responsibility. The government has to stand by parents in safeguarding children's right to life and development. Children in general shall be with their parents. To preserve family unity, children and parents shall be allowed to travel together anywhere. Children shall be protected from abduction.

Every girl and boy, irrespective of territorial boundaries, has the freedom of expression and right to information. Governments shall safeguard their religious freedom and freedom of thinking. Children have the right to mix with others. Both government and society shall provide an environment conducive to their development.

Although bringing up children is the parents' responsibility, the government shall extend its helping hand. Children shall be provided nutritious food and enabled to take part in social activities. They shall not be abused.

Children have the right to education. The government shall provide free and compulsory education. Education shall facilitate the unfolding of the latent talent in children. They shall be protected from ill health and bonded labor. They shall not be sexually abused or subjected to exploitation. Children's rights shall be widely publicized.

The charter is coming to the rescue of victims at some places, but it does not identify religion as one of the causes for the children's plight. It is yet to dawn on the United Nations that tackling symptoms and ignoring the root cause is futile.

What is the contribution of each religion in perpetuating child abuse?

CHRISTIANS

Religion's Crime against Children

Without distinction, all religions have been guilty of gross misbehavior toward children. To begin with, let us study the unpardonable crimes and atrocities committed by Christianity, one of the biggest religions with sway over many developed countries and even the United Nations.

Christianity has many denominations or sects among the Roman Catholics and the Protestants. Almost all denominations abuse children, notwithstanding minor differences.

Sam Harris in his books *Letter to a Christian Nation* and *End of Faith* gave several examples of how Christian denominations have abused human rights. Similar examples have also been amply provided by Richard Dawkins and Christopher Hitchens.

The sects who directly and blatantly harass children are:

> Jehovah's Witnesses
> Christian Science
> Faith Assembly
> The Believers' Fellowship
> Faith Tabernacle
> Church of the First Borne
> Church of God of the Union Assembly
> Church of God Chapel
> Faith Temple Doctoral Church of Christ in God
> Jesus through John and Judy
> Christ Miracle Healing Center
> Northeast Kingdom Community Church
> Christ Assembly
> The Source
> True Followers of Christ
> No Name Fellowship

Most of these are small groups working primarily in the United States. The biggest among them—the Christian Scientists—operates in the United States and Europe.

Their Views Regarding Medical Treatment to Children

A number of these Christian groups preach that medical treatment of sick children is contrary to God's will. Did Christ use drugs for treatment? they ask. Children fall ill because of parents' sins or crimes. A remedy lies in prayer. These groups oppose blood transfusions, injections, and medication. They engender fear of doctors and medicine among Christians.

Despite court verdicts, these parents are subjecting children to faith indoctrination.

Christian Science founder Mary Baker Eddy trots out such arguments in her innumerable writings. The Pentecostal Mission maintains that confessions will cure diseases as they wash away sin, the cause of diseases. Christian devotees belonging to this denomination do not call in doctors or report communicable diseases.

The Christian Science denomination appoints its own nurses and doctors. But they are not trained in modern medicine. They recite devotional songs and Baker Eddy's writings to cure the diseased.

Jehovah's Witnesses' oppose blood transfusions on the grounds that blood contains soul.

Some of these denominations have gone to court and obtained exemptions from medical treatment, which testifies to their clout over courts.

Christian Science founder Mary Eddy Baker went in for corrective eyeglasses for defective vision, got her aching tooth extracted under local anesthesia, and used sedatives to get relief from kidney stones. When this news was leaked, she took the line that devotees could go in for anesthesia and painkillers in the treatment of certain disorders.

There have been innumerable instances of children dying because of these Christian sects' edicts against medical treatment. Children in a developed country like the United States have died of pneumonia, meningitis, diphtheria, appendicitis, diabetes, measles, gangrene, dehydration, blood poisoning, cancer, diarrhea, lung diseases, epilepsy or fits, pericardiatis, hernia, and thalassemia.

Hundreds of children have died in the United States since 1973 because of Christian opposition to medicine, according to details available. One can only imagine the number of deaths that went unreported. CHILD, a nongovernmental organization, has exposed these incidents. CHILD went to court to save some children from certain death and had parents punished for negligence.

When such incidents come to light, the scrutanized denominations maintain that opposition to medical treatment is an aberration of some working in remote areas. Christianity as such should not be blamed, they maintain.

You can only imagine the inhumanity of those who advocate that prayers are the antidotes to diseases like cancer and tetanus and bone fractures. (For details of their inhumanity, see Belle L. Bottoms, Philip R. Shaver, Gall S. Goodman, and Jianjian Qin, "In the Name of God: A Profile of Religion-Related Child Abuse," *Journal of Social Issues* 51, no. 2 [1995].)

Sin in Shroud

The Vatican in Rome, the headquarters of the Roman Catholic Church, is the fountainhead of many evils.

The Church is opposed to marriages between priests and nuns. But since sex is an irresistible human urge, priests and nuns indulge in it behind flowing robes, enjoying religious protection. It is common knowledge that pastors in churches and nuns in convents have sexually assaulted children. Because of social taboos, such instances are not reported. Functionaries ranging from the pope to the ordinary priest or nun have been guilty of misbehavior because of the celibacy ordained by the Catholic Church.

Popes have recognized the religious abuse of children and started taking action against the priests.

Priest Rudolph Kos of Dallas, Texas, admitted to having raped Nathan Nicholas, a boy assisting him in church rituals. It was revealed the priest abused ten boys for a period of eleven years. Rudolph Kos abused the boys for massage, masturbation, and oral sex, sometimes after administering sedatives.

When the Rudolph Kos sex scandal broke out for the first time in 1992, the church suspended him. But the Church, which lost its case in court, appealed the decision. Bishop Charles Grahmann contended that Kos had taken the Church for a ride, too. They lost the appeal and $119.6 million. Since the money belonged to the public, there was none to question it. Jay Lemberger, a boy who assisted Kos in church rituals, committed suicide. The court directed the Church to pay a compensation of $20.2 million to the boy's parents.

The Catholic Church remains indifferent when children are thus exploited. Occasionally it takes token action like transferring the guilty religious official. Because of the Roman Catholic Church's greater level of dictatorship than in Protestant, Methodist, Lutheran, and Baptist churches, it would not allow sexual exploitation instances to come to light. Parents are gradually mustering courage to expose the guilty.

Instances in Europe

There have been instances of Catholic priests in Europe indulging in sexual crimes against children.

In 1995, seventy-eight-year-old Austrian Cardinal Hans Hermann was found guilty of raping boys. When victims and colleagues exposed him, the Catholic Church relieved him of his duties. The cardinal confessed to his crime. The *New York Times* published the news on April 15, 1998, shortly before the pope's visit to Austria.

Seventy-year-old priest Brinden Smith of Ireland was sentenced to four years in jail for sexually abusing children for thirty-six years.

In the Irish Protestant-Catholic clashes, children were also fielded in the name of religion.

Researchers have published many books and articles on the abuse of children and underlined the need to keep children away from religion. (See the appendix for references.)

Losing her child to religious atrocities, Rita Swan of the United States got out of religion and started an organization, CHILD, to rescue children. Besides collecting details of children who died as a result of religious violence, she has also been successfully fighting battles for them in courts of law.

In Europe, Radda Barnen founded a child rights institution and published many books. The United Nations has recognized the institution's commendable work.

The civilized world has expressed its shock over Christian violence on children. There has also been a flood of criticism of the Church. Yet the Church remains unruffled. The Church paid huge amounts through courts and out-of-court settlements, but still they have not gotten to the root of the problem.

The Bible and Children

Christians' scripture, the Bible, preaches love, compassion, forgiveness, and other values. Yet when it comes to children, it changes its tune. Proverbs in the Bible talk about the need for corporal punishment in the interest of the child. Refraining from beating is tantamount to hating, says one proverb. Cane rescues the soul from hell, says another (Proverbs 13:24, 23:13–14). Devout Christians who believe that the Bible contains the ultimate truth do not find anything wrong in punishing children. Teachers thrash children in the name of driving Satan out from them.[7]

There is a constant conflict between science and the Bible, both of which children study. Where there is a conflict, children are advised to ignore science and blindly believe the scripture. Their curiosity is stifled as they are prevented from questioning. If the miracles in the Bible are narrated as fiction, nobody has any objection. Children can read, enjoy, and forget the stories. No harm befalls them. The trouble only arises when they are advised to believe and practice what they are taught are facts.

Christians, who condemned Galileo for centuries, today confess they were wrong. The pope has officially declared so. As per the Bible, the earth is flat and is the center of the universe, and the sun revolves round the earth. Science established that the Bible version was a cock-and-bull story.

Christians question Darwin's theory of evolution and want the story of God's creation to be taught, citing Bible as proof.

Christians forget that there are two theories of creation in the initial chapters of the Bible. Children should not question which of them is correct.

Bible Contradictions

Children are confused by several contradictions in the Bible. In Genesis, the first two chapters have many contradictory statements. For example:

God Created man in his own image.

2. Lord God formed man of the dust on the ground and
   Male and female created by Him.
   Breathed into his nostril, the
   breath of life. God took a rib
   of man and made women out
   of it.

Five hundred contradictions were shown by William Henry Burr in his book *Self Contradictions of the Bible*.

Children should believe that Eve was created out of Adam's rib bone. Children notice the discrepancy between the origin of life learned scientifically and the Bible's strange concoction. Yet they should remain silent.

They should not ask whether God lied when he warned Adam and Eve against eating the forbidden fruit because of its deadly effect. They should not inquire why Adam and Eve, who ate the fruit at the insistence of Satan, did not die. In what language did Satan in snake-form speak? Who created Satan and why? All such queries are quelled with the cane. Children have to believe the story that fearing the birth of Christ, King Herod ordered the killing of all children.

There is the story of a father complying with the wish of God for his son's sacrifice. What is the moral of the story for children?

Should children believe that Christ resurrected a dead Lazarus on the third day after his death to console his mother? Did Lazarus live subsequently? Did he die again? Why did Christ resurrect only Lazarus? Did Lazarus recount his experiences after death to anybody? The news would have spread like wildfire and thousands of people would have congregated to see a dead man coming to life. How is it that the Bible does not contain any more details about him? It is natural for children to raise such queries.

In fact there were four new testaments written by John, Matthew, Luke, and Mark. But only John's testament records the miracle. Children naturally like to know why the other three did not write about it.

Mary was said to have given birth to Christ as a virgin. Jesus is said to be the Son of God, described as Holy Ghost. Although the story cannot be proven, children have to believe it unquestioningly.

Noah's Ark was said to have saved animals, birds, and insects. A modern student will be assailed by umpteen different doubts. Did the carnivores and herbivores aboard lead a peaceful coexistence? Did goats and tigers play together? If carnivores had eaten the deer, goats, and sheep, which animals were left behind? Would not the boat have sprung a leak and sunk had a borer bird chipped away the wood? Could a panda of China, a kangaroo of Australia, an iguana of South America, a polar bear of the arctic, and a shark of the ocean have all been collected? How did Noah's family withstand the stink of feces discharged by the animals? Children should not raise such embarrassing questions.

The Bible talks of many unsavory things like father-daughter incest, prostitution, murder, and other atrocities. Would not children feel repulsed if they were made to recite the Bible in the name of devotion?

Children should be clearly taught what is fact and what is fiction.

Isaac Asimov studied the Bible and recorded his scientific findings. At the instance of the British King James, the Bible was modernized and published in an easy-to-read style.

Was Mother Teresa involved in child abuse?

Yes, of course.

Mother Teresa's attitude toward destitute children is classic example of child abuse by Catholic nuns. Dr. Fox Robin, editor of the *Lancet*, a British medical magazine, revealed how the syringes are washed in cold water in Mother Teresa's institutes in Kolkata, India.[8]

Dr. Aroup Chatterjee in his book *The Final Verdict*[9] thoroughly exposed the firsthand experiences of Mother Teresa's attitude toward children and her cruel treatment of them while they suffered with ailments. Her only treatment is "prayer" as a panacea. Christopher Hitchens, a writer and journalist, and Mr. Tariq Ali, a writer, have shown to the world through documentaries (*Hell's Angel*) and writings how Mother Teresa behaved toward destitute children, which is a telling example of child abuse by religious Catholics.

MUSLIMS

Islam and Children

The world over, Muslim children undergo abuse in the name of religion. American Muslims take their female children often on foreign trips. It is not for pleasure. It is to subject them to genital mutilation, or circumcision (*sunna*), which they believe is a good religious practice. American law does not permit female circumcisions. UNICEF noticed that Muslims in twenty-eight countries spread over Africa and Asia practice circumcision.

Fanatic Muslims who insist on Islamic practice indulge in such abuse by traveling abroad, where they can have circumcision performed on their children without any legal inhibition.

UNICEF calls it a wrong cultural practice instead of condemning it as an obscurantist religious perversion. Perhaps UNICEF does not want to offend Muslims.

Muslims, for reasons unknown, believe that a girl's clitoris should be excised. They don't cite any scientific reason for their belief. Nurses or quacks carry out the procedure with a razor blade or scissors, without administering anesthesia. Girls who have undergone the procedure have died of septicemia, tetanus, hemorrhage, sepsis, and AIDS.

Ayaan Hirsi Ali in her book *Infidel* and Christopher Hitchens in his book *God Is Not Great* gave instances of children undergoing such sufferings.

In some instances, circumcisions have resulted in difficult sex, problems during pregnancy, urinary tract infections, and menstrual troubles.

UNICEF wants the antediluvian circumcision practice to be done away with, as it infringes on children's rights.

Why do Muslims believe in circumcision? According to Muslim pundits themselves, the Koran does not prescribe it as mandatory. Yet mullahs and clerics approve of it and regard opponents as antireligious. The fight is on in Egypt between fundamentalists and modernists on this issue. In Somalia, 98 percent of Muslim girls are subjected to circumcision.[10]

Some imams say that drawing blood with the prick of a needle can be a substitute for circumcision. This is to implement the Islamic practice.

Muslim women's organizations are opposed to the perpetuation of this practice, but they are too weak to end it. UNICEF, trying to end the malpractice through education, distributes first aid kits to girls undergoing circumcision!

Koran Recitation

Muslims the world over invariably make their children memorize the Koran. Children are sent to schools run by mullahs in mosques. They are taught how to recite the 6,200 suras written in Arabic. The children may be illiterate, ignorant of Arabic and the meaning of what they are told to know by heart. Yet they blindly memorize.

Taslima Nasrin, the famous Bengali author from Bangladesh, wrote about memorizing the Koran in her book, *My Girlhood*:

> When Ma ordered me to do my namaaz, I washed my hands at the tubewell, covered my head, bowed, bent my knees, then knelt down as required, and muttered the Arabic words I had been taught without understanding their meaning. One day I said to Ma, "My teachers in school say I shouldn't learn anything by heart without learning what it means. Only stupid students learn their lessons by heart and write them out, word for word. Intelligent students grasp the meaning of a lesson, then write what they've learnt in their *own* words. In this case, Ma, if we prayed in Bengali instead of Arabic, why should that matter? Surely Allah can understand our language as well?"
>
> "Shut up, you talk too much!" Ma hissed in fury. "Don't give me more grief, please. How I hoped that my girl, born on a holy day, would turn out to be virtuous, do her namaaz, observe roja. But . . ." her voice trailed away. She avoided my question altogether.

Reposing faith in the Holy Scripture, children are not expected to raise any queries.

There is not one aspect of the Koran on which all Muslims agree. There are versions with different interpretations.

Ibn Warraq published volumes about different versions of the Koran followed by Sunnis, Shias, and other sects. This led to conflicts, as well.

Muslims are also divided on how to pronounce vowels and consonants. This confuses all children.

What do the children learn from the Koran? They are told that women are inferior to men, contrary to the generally accepted line that women and men are equal. When there is a conflict between human rights and the Koran, mullahs say the Koran cannot be questioned. Boys brought up this way thus develop a superiority complex and start looking down on girls.

Muslims practice child marriages, citing the Koran. Muhammad himself married six-year-old Ayesha. Ayesha joined Muhammad as a spouse in her ninth year. This marriage is cited often to justify child marriages. A Muslim girl's consent is not necessary for marriage. Unlike the civilized world, Islam does not consider sex with children a crime.

This Is Religious Culture

What is the impact of such practices on children? Muslims violently retaliate if Muhammad is criticized or condemned. So most people remain mute out of fear.

According to Muslim tradition, killing of soldiers captured in a campaign is not a crime. So is the sale of women and children as slaves. Islam approved and encouraged slavery, contrary to the civilized world's view that slavery in all forms is reprehensible.

Similar things in the Old Testament are vividly explained by Richard Dawkins in his *The God Delusion* as well as by Robert Ingersoll in his lectures and essays.

Muhammad married the wife of his adopted son. She had been divorced earlier. Otherwise, the Koran would not approve of one's marriage with a daughter-in-law. A slave by the name of Jayad—part of the dowry received by Muhammad on his marriage—later became his adopted son. His wife Janab was a beauty. Muhammad liked her, and the adopted son divorced her. With religious and legal hurdles out of the way, Muhammad married Janab and said he had carried out Allah's wishes. Muhammad knew that no one could stop him if he invoked Allah's name.

Muslim boys, who think girls are inferior to them, want girls to wear purdahs. A number of Muslim societies and governments have been repressing women for centuries, although women in some places have revolted and rose to become prime ministers. It may take a long time for Muslim women to assert their rights; neither parents, nor teachers, nor mullahs dispel students' natural doubts over the Koran. They unleash threats or thrashings to make the children comply.

What do the children learn? Cruel punishment visits those committing adultery and other crimes. Inflicting one hundred whip lashes in public is one such punishment. The victims are badly crippled or they die. Pelting with stones to death is the punishment for adultery. The judge pronounces one guilty, based on the evidence of four witnesses, giving no opportunity to the accused to defend or produce witnesses. The hearing is one-sided. Swearing by the Koran, the judge is unconcerned about human rights. The woman found guilty is buried up to the neck. Spectators follow the judge and the witnesses in stoning the accused to death.

Children are terrified with such punishments, and it will have deep impact on their thinking and behavior.

Children have to keep quiet when the father beats up the mother, as the Koran confers such a right on husbands. He can thrash her if she refuses to go to bed even on grounds of ill health. But the wife can never reply in the same way.

As per Muslim law, men can easily divorce their wives by uttering the word "talaq" three times. In contrast, it is very difficult for women to divorce spouses.

Children who read about Muhammad's four marriages and some divorces believe the Koran sanctions these.

Taslima Nasrin, a Muslim from Bangladesh with a fatwa on her head, tells of child abuse in her book *My Girlhood*:

WRONG PREACHINGS

I had just found the Quran in Bengali and was reading it, licking a little ball of tamarind from time to time. What I read froze my blood. The moon has its own light, it said. The earth always stands still. If it does not lean on one side it is because all the mountains, acting like nails, are holding it in place.

I read these words over and over, first tilting my neck to the left, then tilting it to the right as I re-read them. How was this possible? The earth did not stand still, it moved around the sun.

Could the Quran have made a mistake or was what I had been taught in school wrong?

I felt very confused.

Was there no such thing as gravity? Was the earth really held in place by mountains? My science books told me that the earth rotates once every twenty-four hours; that meant it was moving all the time!

Which was true? Science or the Quran?

The tamarind remained suspended in my hand—I forgot to eat it. Completely taken aback I sat on the floor with outstretched legs, the book open on my knees. Strong gusts of hot wind came in through the open windows making the blue curtains flutter, lifting my hair and the pages of my book. My mind also took flight. It rose higher and higher in the sky, getting larger and larger while my body seemed to shrink to the point of completely ceasing to exist. I remained where I was like a dot, helpless and immobile. The sound of a dove calling in the distance brought me back to my senses. My eyes began to move once more and I read on:

Man's female companion has been created from one of his ribs. One of the bones in a woman's neck is crooked, that is why no woman thinks straight or walks on a straight path. Women are like a field for growing crops, men are totally free to go when and where they like. If a woman is disobedient, her husband has the right to drive her away from his bed, then he may try to talk some sense into her, but if she remains disobedient he can beat her. Women can claim only one-third of any property owned by their fathers. Men can claim two-thirds. Men can take one, two, three, even four wives. Women have no such right. Men can divorce their wives simply by uttering the word "talaq!" three times. Women are not allowed to seek a divorce at all. When acting as witnesses to an event, two women are counted as one witness, whereas every single man is a complete witness.

In all this I was prepared to make allowances for what was said about the earth and the moon. All right, I was in no position to say for sure whether the moon had its own source of light, or whether the earth moved or remained still. I had seen nothing for myself. But how could there be such difference between men and women? Once,

Chhotda and I had peeped into the room of a medical student in our neighbourhood and had seen a human skeleton in it. Chhotda told me that it could have been either a man's or a woman's, it was impossible to tell. There were two hundred and six bones in the human body. My teachers in school said the same thing. I could spot no difference between Dada's neck and mine—his was as straight as my own! He was in the habit of cracking not just his knuckles, but whatever else he could. He jerked his head sometimes from side to side, making cracking noises. Then he would stretch his whole body and some of the bones in his back would creak. He didn't stop there—there were times when he pushed me against a wall and pressed my neck. The bones in my neck made an identical noise. As for ribs, I had as many as he, Ma had as many as Baba. Strictly speaking, Baba ought to have one less since Ma was supposed to have been made from it. What if a man had four wives? Would he lose four ribs? I couldn't believe it. Nana had married a second woman and lived with her for a couple of weeks. Had she, too, been made from one of Nana's ribs?

Why should anyone need two women to act as one witness, when the word of a single man was considered sufficient? Didn't women speak the truth? Were only men honest and truthful?

The Koran engenders fear and concern about life in hell. The children are taught that people like liars, infidels, and drunkards go to hell. The fear continues to haunt them throughout their lives.

How Muslim children are brainwashed with blind faith is narrated by Taslima Nasrin. Here is another interesting passage from *My Girlhood*:

I failed to see what I had said that was so objectionable. I just wanted Ma to see that a child has no power to decide where it will be born and which faith it will adopt. Since that decision is made by Allah, the final responsibility for the child's future must also rest with him. But Ma didn't want to burden Allah with difficult or complex responsibilities. Her list of "dislikes" and things she disapproved of grew so long that no matter what I said, I always seemed to be committing a sin.

One day Ma saw me standing by the tubewell, drinking water out of a glass. "Why are you drinking water standing up? If you do that, it means you're drinking the devil's urine," she told me. When I returned after a trip to the toilet, she examined my hands to see if they were damp or dry. If they were dry, she said, "Did you wash your hands after doing your business? Hindus don't. The right place for those kafirs is in hell."

There was a fragrant *hasnuhana* plant outside a window in my room, facing east. All night, its sweet scent filled the air but if I tried sleeping with my head under that window, Ma shouted at me, "Why are you lying there with your feet pointing west? Don't you know that's where Kabah-Sharif lies? It's a sin to point your feet at it. Turn around; sleep with your head to the west.

By this time I had learnt to recognize the four directions. When Ma pointed west, it suddenly occurred to me that a Hindu temple stood here. But I knew that if I mentioned that, Ma would call me the Devil's advocate and quite possibly, punch my back. So, rather meekly, I moved my feet away from Mecca and Kabah-sharif, although thousands of miles separated my poor feet from those holy places and in the interviewing space, lay mountains, lakes, rivers, lavatories, temples, churches—everything.

I could find no logic in Ma's religious beliefs. When I asked questions, I received some very simple answers, the gist of which was this: Allah had made humans with clay and jinns with fire. Every spirit, be it human or jinn, would one day be judged in Hashar, the field of Judgment. Where did jinns live? They remained invisible but they were there, hiding in the air. Where did Allah live? Allah was light, the source of creation. He, too, was invisible; He lived somewhere up in the sky. But no matter where he was he could see and hear everything.

Ma said all that, but on the night of shab-e-barrat, having made kheer and others dishes and arranged for prayers to continue all night, Ma also said, "Today, Allah is going to come down from seventh heaven, he is going to look closely at what's going on in the world."

Children amid Minefields

Some countries fighting wars in the name of religion (jihad) rope in children by giving them military training. Children who should be in schools are dragged to theaters of war.

The United Nations has called for measures to safeguard children in times of war and take care of them if injured. Children are maimed or killed when they step on land mines laid as part of war in places like Cambodia, Bosnia, Afghanistan, Iraq, Central America, and Africa. Under the Taliban regime in Afghanistan, land mines have killed children going to school, playing, or carrying out chores like collecting firewood and fetching water. It is estimated that there are fifteen million mines in Angola and ten million in Iraq. Thirty percent of the accidents involve children.

Every year ten thousand children are killed or disabled by land mines in the world. Many countries have agreed on the need for a ban on laying land mines in the future. The International Labor Organization, a wing of the United Nations, published these figures, and every year they are updated.

Deactivation of the existing mines is an expensive proposition.

There should be a ban on inciting children to join wars.

The Taliban recruited children in Afghanistan during early 1990s for the holy war against the West in the name of religion. While politicians invoke religion to serve their selfish ends, priests and mullahs back them by quoting scripture.

The UN has taken up the task of educating children about landmines and ways of avoiding them. The UN needs the cooperation of national governments in making the campaign a success. Religion and state should be separated. Children under no circumstances should be dragged into conflicts.

Only forty-four countries have adopted legislation against domestic violence and twenty-seven countries against sexual violence. Although children have been conferred rights by the UN in 1989, they are yet to be enforced. Even the United States has yet to adopt the Children's Charter.

Older Muslim men from the Gulf countries marry young Indian Muslim girls after paying off the girls' parents, and they are taken home to be used as slaves. Mullahs keep quiet, turning a blind eye to the fact and do not take to task the khajis or priests who perform these marriages.

Child victims of such atrocities are growing in number every year. The civilized world should take note of them.

Human Rights and Islam

The first article of the human rights charter says that all human beings are equal, have equal discriminating faculties, and should live in brotherhood.

The Koran says that men and women are not equal. In law, a woman's evidence is equal to only 50 percent of a man's evidence. Muslim women cannot marry non-Muslims.

The second article says that all should enjoy equal right to freedom irrespective of race, color, language, religion, politics, or gender.

But in Muslim countries human rights are not extended to non-Muslims. In Saudi Arabia, for instance, Hindus and Christians cannot construct temples or churches or hold public religious functions. But Muslims can build mosques in other countries, say their prayers, and observe their religious rituals in public.

According to the third article, all have a right to life, liberty, and security.

In Muslim countries, atheists are not tolerated. Islam says that killing them is not wrong, maintaining that atheism is a greater crime than adultery, theft, or murder.

According to the human rights charter, slavery and bonded labor are unacceptable.

But the Koran approves slavery and sex with women slaves.

According to the human rights charter, inhumane and cruel punishments are not permitted.

Koran-based Muslim law, in contrast, prescribes flogging, pelting with stones, fracturing/amputation of hands and legs, burial up to the neck, and so on as punishments.

A Muslim cannot change his religion. One who gives up Islam can be sentenced to death. But others are permitted to convert to Islam.

According to the human rights charter, everyone should enjoy the freedom of thought and expression.

In Islamic countries, such freedom is not allowed. Even Muslim minorities like Shias, Ahmediyas, Bahais, and Khurds go through untold hardship, not to mention non-Muslims.

Although they are signatories, Muslim countries do not honor the human rights charter. Children learn about the rights only to keep their mouths shut.

Taliban Abuses

Afghanistan came under Taliban rule in 1996 after liberation from twenty years of cruel Russian control. Reigning over most of the country, the Taliban converted the people into flocks. In the name of following Islam to the letter, it drove women and children into the pre-historic age. Women who did not cover themselves up in purdahs were beaten up. Girls were confined to homes with the closure of schools. Taliban cadres, who underwent training on Pakistan's borders, took cudgels against modern civilization. They brought children under control by brandishing knives or guns and then used them in wars. Human rights organizations raised a furor over the way women and children were treated in Afghanistan. Even some Muslim countries were shocked by these acts.

Talibanization was a term coined following the rise of the Taliban movement in Afghanistan referring to the process were other religious groups or movements come to follow or imitate the strict practices of the Taliban. In its original usage, Talibanization referred to groups who followed Taliban practices such as:

- Strict regulation of women, including forbidding most employment or schooling for women
- The banning of long lists of activities generally tolerated by other Muslims—movies, television, videos, music, dancing, hanging pictures in homes, clapping during sports events
- The banning of activities (especially hairstyles and clothing) generally tolerated by other Muslims on the grounds that the activities are Western
- Oppression of Shia, including takfir threats, that they either convert to Sunni Islam or be prepare to be killed
- Aggressive enforcement of its regulations, particularly the use of armed "religious police"
- The destruction of non-Muslim artifacts, especially carvings and statues such as Buddhas of Bamyan, generally tolerated by other Muslims, on the grounds that the artifacts are idolatrous or Shirk (polytheism)
- Harboring of Al Qaeda or other Islamic militia operatives
- A discriminatory attitude toward non-Muslims such as Taliban-enacted sumptuary laws against Afghan Hindus, requiring them to wear yellow badges, a practice that reminded some of Nazi Germany's anti-Semitic policies. The term was first used to describe areas or groups outside of Afghanistan that came under the influence of the Taliban, such as the area of Waziristan in Pakistan.
- Girls and boys are segregated in the schools, and later, girls are prohibited to educate themselves in schools.

Costly Criticism

How should children react to criticism of the Koran, Muhammad, and Islam? In many countries, critics of Islam are killed, jailed, or abused.

Children realize that Islamic mullahs resort to trials of strength and violence when they cannot rebut critics.

Islam has played a pivotal role in history. The credit for handing over Greek and Roman civilizations, arts, history, and sciences to Europe goes to Muslims. But Islam never displayed religious tolerance. After successful military campaigns, Muslim invaders cruelly killed the captured and sold women and children as slaves. Children would never like to follow a religion that approves of slavery, polygamy, and cruel punishments. That is why Islam seeks to forcibly mold children. Shielding children from science, it drowns them in superstitions. Parents and elders show the way to children by practicing male superiority and repression of women.

Mental Abuse

Fear and anxiety are systematically etched in children's minds. Fear is the bedrock of the Koran's morals.

While Allah is portrayed as kind and compassionate, children are taught about the killing of adversaries and experiences in hell if one goes against Islam. If God has predetermined everything, children cannot comprehend why some are condemned to hell. Does God decide a priori on sending people to hell? How can such a God be a personification of compassion and love? wonder children.

The punishments mentioned in Koran run counter to modern civilization. According to sura 5:38, the punishment for the first offense of theft is amputation of hands and for the second, amputation of legs. The offender is then jailed. Sura 5:33 lists beating, amputation, killing, and deportation among the punishments for opponents of God and his messengers. Sura 4:15 says that women found guilty of adultery on the basis of four witnesses have to be kept under lifelong house arrest. Sura 24:2–4 prescribes one hundred whiplashes for prostitution.

One finds two sets of suras with contradictory views. In the earlier version there is religious tolerance. Faith and rituals are left to individuals with no element of compulsion. "Wish peace of mind to those who do not believe in your religion or God," say some suras. Suras 10:9, 50:45, 2:256, and 2:62 exemplify these thoughts.

In contrast, suras like 2, 4, 5, 8, 9, 22, and 47 exemplify religious intolerance, cruel punishments, and killings. Suras 22:9 and 47:4 make it plain that the Koran does not show tolerance toward nonbelievers.

The Koran calls for waging a religious war called jihad until the entire world is brought under Islam. Worshippers of other religions have to be eliminated (see suras 2:256, 4:74, 4:76, 8:12, 8:15, 8:39–42, 9:5–6, 9:39, and 16).

Those who surrender in Muslim campaigns are called Thimmas or slaves, and they do not enjoy any rights. Taxes like "kharab" and "jijia" are extracted from them. Islam does not agree that all are equal in the eyes of law.

Children are taught these things in religious seminaries called madrassas. Thus early seeds of hatred toward other religions and belief in Islam is instilled among the children. Hence they are not able to come out of that early influence even though they study science and technology later in their life. Some of the terrorist participants are well educated but that does not prevent them from undertaking terrorist activities.

These suras are a sure sign of how indoctrination of children stunts their growth.

Koran and Science

Contradictions between the Koran and science confront the modern student. Should a student follow the Koran and keep the faith, or science, which is founded in research, proof, evidence, and mathematics? The Koran cannot withstand scientific scrutiny. While the world revolves around science, the Muslim world cannot reconcile itself to science. That is why many Muslims keep science aside.

If one follows the Koran, one has to extend unusual respect to the moon and believe in unscientific things. The moon is not self-evanescent. Man has set foot on the moon and brought back rocks. The believers in the Koran find it incredible (see sura 10:5).

Mullahs maintain that the Koran is a treasure trove of wisdom. They try in vain to discover in the Koran what science has already unraveled.

The Koran maintains that Allah created the universe in six days. The Koran says that God's throne was floating on water, Adam was created out of earth, and the moon was created to measure time.

Believers assert that the Koran talked of cross-pollination long before scientists did. They try to defend that Adam's creation out of earth is scientific.

According to the Koran, the earth came into existence prior to heaven (sura 14:12). The sun revolves around the earth. The Koran makes no sense to those who study the modern theories of evolution and astronomy.

According to mullahs, science means only their religious traditions and customs. They dismiss modern science as antireligious and alien. Because of such fundamentalism, Muslim students in general continue to remain very backward in sciences.

A devout Muslim student of the Koran is bound to wonder how a kindly Allah could be responsible for droughts and famines, earthquakes and tidal waves, floods and hailstorms.

The Koran's theory of creation cannot withstand the scientific theory of evolution enunciated by Darwin and others. If a student believes in the creation of Adam and Eve, it is only because of fear from mullahs.

Koran's Heaven of Sexual Ecstasy

Many suras in the Koran vividly describe how human beings enjoy sex in heaven. Should children memorize such verses? The consensus now is that children be kept away from sexual matters until they come of age. There are demands that children be denied access to pornography on the Internet. Does it become sacred simply because it is found in the Koran? (See suras 2:25, 37:38–49, 38:49–53, 44:51–55, 45:70–74, 46:10–22, 52:19–20, 55:54–58, 56:35–38, 78:31–33.) The Koran treats women as second-rate citizens and portrays them as enjoyable commodities in heaven. Such an attitude reflecting male superiority, arrogance, and selfishness is opposed to human rights.

The Koran is said to contain ultimate truths. Doubting or questioning them is criminal, say the mullahs. How can children believe in things that are opposed to human rights, equality, freedom, and scientific research?

Children should, therefore, be kept away from the Koran and given the freedom to pursue their own path once they grow up.

Shia Muslims in Iran, who came to power through the 1980 Iranian revolution, have imposed severe restrictions on women in the name of the Koran. Women have to wear the purdah and cannot ride bicycles like men. The women who took part in the revolution were deeply disappointed. Some are still fighting for their rights and withstanding their hardships. Some women who became ministers after getting elected to parliament are trying to break the Islamic stranglehold to ensure equal rights for women.

To learn more about the efforts underway in the field, see publications of Sisterhood's Global Institute, "Safe & Secure: Eliminating Violence against Women and Girls in Muslim Societies," (Bethesda, MD) and Haleh Esfandiari's *Reconstructed Lives—Women & Iran's Islamic Revolution* (Johns Hopkins University Press, 1997). Wlumi Documentation details how women and children are subjected to abuse in the name of the Koran and Islam all over the world.

Muslims account for one-fourth of the world's population and many countries are under Islamic rule. Muslim traditions, customs, and religious scriptures have assumed importance as they clash with democracy, human rights, and science. In the name of jihad, some Muslims have degenerated into terrorists and indulged in killing people. Even children are fed on fanaticism.

HINDUS

Since the Vedic age, higher-caste Brahmins and Kshatriyas sent their children to ashram schools for studies. The caste system (called Varna) created four castes. The upper castes—namely, Brahmins and ruling-class Kshatriyas—could undergo available education in forest seminaries. The privilege was denied to other castes. The four-level caste system also created the untouchable caste, whose members were forced to live outside villages and to serve villagers. This gradation continued for centuries and was sanctified through religion.

Buddha rebelled against the Hindu caste system and untouchability. He also gave equal rights to women along with men, which was not possible in Hindu society. Children of Hindu castes imbibed this treatment that inhibited the personal growth of many.

Saints and sages living in cottages beside rivers or rivulets or on the outskirts of villages or forests got support from the villages. The children spent years in these cottages doing domestic chores and grazing the cattle of teachers while learning. (Lower-caste children had no right to education.)

Education meant recitation of mantras and withstanding memory tests. Teachers meted out punishment to them in the name of discipline. Children often pined for their parents, as they could look them up only once or twice during their ten-year stay in the ashram. Literature is full of instances of the teacher and his wife sexually assaulting children. The "Chandogyaupanishad" and "Manusmrithi" warn teachers to beware of students likely to indulge in adultery with their wives. The teacher did not begin teaching Satyakama Jabali until she attained twelve years.

The Upanishads are traditional religious books of Hindus. Similarly, Hindu law was codified by Manu, and he prescribed different punishments to different castes even if the crime was the same. B. R. Ambedkar, the head of the Indian Constitution, condemned Manu code as barbaric and gave a call to the people to burn it publicly.

During the Upanishad times bonded labor flourished, unhindered in the name of education in ashram schools. Students were made to beg and fetch ingredients for rituals. Those who studied in ashram schools became priests. Whether they understood the meaning of the mantras or not, people called in priests for every function.

Ashram schools followed the caste order in the name of dharma.

If a lower-caste student like Ekalavya excelled like higher-caste children in archery, a teacher like Dronacharya sought his thumb to checkmate him.

Children were taught untouchability. Children of the village should not touch or interact with children of the untouchable castes that were kept outside the village. God's name was invoked to justify such caste discrimination. Caste feelings were promoted among those in the village.

Girls were looked down upon. They were not sent to ashram schools as they were meant for domestic work. Vedas were taboo for women.

The caste system is religious in that it has its roots and sanctions in the holy books of Hindus. They are Vedas and Gita. Hence a Hindu is born into a caste and cannot change it willingly. The holy book Gita says thus:

Hindu Caste System

The four castes were created by me, according to the apportionment of qualities (or modes) and works. Know that I, the uncreating and unchanging, am the creator of them.

—Gita (IV–13)

It should now be clear that what Krishna meant was not "the four-fold order" (a single unit) but the four castes (four different and rigid entities). A Hindu is born into a caste; he lives and dies as a member of that caste, and even his life after death depends on the zeal and devotion with which he had discharged the duties of his caste during his lifetime. There is no scope whatsoever for social mobility, and in particular, for vertical mobility. In a class society a man may be the son of a labourer, but that would not preclude him from rising to the status of a lord, spiritual or temporal; nothing of the kind is possible in the caste system.

Krishna does not deny his responsibility for the iniquitous system; on the contrary, he owns it as his own creation. But here, too, he shows his genius for equivocation. On the one hand, Krishna claims that he fixes the caste status of each man in strict accordance with that man's good or evil deeds in previous birth or births, and the temperament which those deeds invested him with, and on the other hand, Krishna declares, "I am non-agent; I am immutable." He may or may not have been the Lord of the *Jagat* (Universe) but he was certainly the Lord of Jugglery.

Taking their cue from the Lord of Jugglery, the commentators on the Gita maintain that the caste system is not man-made but god-made; it is "therefore" sacrosanct. To attack it is to show defiance of god, to undermine it is to sabotage what is a god-ordained social order. To be sure, it is an order based on the high and the low, the underprivileged millions at the bottom. But then, god is only nominally the creator of the system; it is, in fact, the past karma of men that creates the system. The role of the god is confined to deciding the caste of each man according to his natural aptitudes, his pronounced proclivities, his Swabhava. How can the Swabhava of a man be known before his birth? But is not God all-seeing, all-knowing? And so, he can decide the Swabhava of a man even before he enters the womb of his mother. Indeed, all the previous births of the man yet to be conceived, and yet to take birth, are fully known to God. Did not Krishna tell Arjuna, "I know all your past births, you don't" (IX–5).

Child marriages were the norm and justified in the name of god. Marriages were made in heaven, they argued. Some became widows in childhood but widow marriages were banned. Child widows were looked down upon.

Sati—in which a wife joins her dead husband on the funeral pyre—was practiced as dharma. Women were thus forcibly burnt.

Such atrocities were committed in the name of Hindu religion. Holy scripture was quoted to make the public believe that they were all God's decisions. Indoctrination from childhood turned people into mental slaves.

We are delving into the religious past because it strongly influences social customs and traditions even to this day, notwithstanding modern education.

In India, there are two streams of religious traditions. Brahmins and Kshatriyas follow the traditions of the Vedas, Upanishads, Darsanas, and other religious works. Vysyas and Sudras try to imitate them. It is called great tradition. Vedas are written in Sanskrit language and they are four in number. Lower castes like Vysyas and Sudras are prohibited from reading these holy books. The books have become the monopoly of Brahmins.

The lower tradition, represented by Puranas and Itihasas, is meant for the masses. All motley gods are attributed to the masses. Thus religion segregates people even in worship, sacrifices, and traditions. Children also follow the same gradations.

Hindus cleverly made Buddha as one of Hindu incarnation and thus killed Buddhism in India.

Sacrifice of human beings and animals continued as a religious tradition. Although they came to a halt when the Buddha stridently opposed the practice, they were revived later with a vengeance. By co-opting the Buddha, Hinduism camouflaged its traditions and survived.

Lower-caste children who were devoid of education lived in slavery or bonded labor. Parents did not feel anything wrong in treating their children as property and living off of their labor.

We have to recall history because of calls for revival of ashram schools and teaching of Hindu dharma to children.

Whatever was taught in ashram schools was unscientific and stifled children's thinking, inquisitiveness, and questioning.

All ancient astrology is contrary to astronomy. Yet astrology, palmistry, and vastu are followed to this day. People are asked to continue to believe what they did once for want of proof. Among such is the belief in the ten reincarnations of god. Although contrary to the theory of evolution, the ten reincarnations continue to be worshipped.

Children are taught these blind beliefs like geomancy, astrology, reincarnation, and rebirth, all of which kill their spirit of inquiry, their quest for knowledge. Questioning and searching for truth is discouraged. When there is conflict between religious belief and scientific fact, children are asked to follow religion with veneration. That is awful abuse.

Should children be taught scriptures that extend the caste order to animals, birds, and even planets? According to the scriptures, Jupiter and Venus are Brahmins, Mars and sun are Kshatriyas—that the sun is not a planet is not known to our astrology—Buddha a Vysya, and Saturn a Sudra. Animal features are attributed to stars.

We cannot inflict greater cruelty on children than teaching them dharma sastras. How can children be taught caste divisions and superiority and inferiority among human beings in these days of respect for human rights and equality?

Children are segregated in castes even in schools. Until British rule is over in India, such practice was continued. The untouchable community children are allotted separate space in classrooms.

Into the New Millennium

In India, the dead weight of the past is crippling children. Parents leave a legacy of their blind beliefs, superstitions, and evil practices to their children. These vary from state to state. Children learn about Sati practice in Rajastan. Sati is burning the wife along with the husband on pyre. When the husband dies, the traditional Hindu custom is preached that a wife has no life and should die along with her husband. This practice was mentioned in Hindu holy books and it was banned during British rule in India. Yet there are instances in states like Rajastan where Sati is still practiced. Children naturally undergo traumatic experiences with such Hindu practices. Fortunately, it is not very popular nowadays.

The places of Sati are treated as sacred, and temples are constructed in Rajastan state, near Delhi!

In Andhra Pradesh State

Child marriages were the norm even at the beginning of the twentieth century. Many girls became widows in their childhood and withered away wearing white saris and covering their tonsured heads. Child marriages were performed invoking religion, fatalistic theories about birth, and prospects of a better life in heaven. While a priest recited mantras and made the bridegroom tie the sacred wedding thread, elders feasted and blessed the couple, not thinking in the very least of the bleak future awaiting the children.

There are laws against child marriages but often they are observed in breach.

Social reformer and writer Gurazada Apparao's heart-rending narration of young married girls ending their lives by plunging into wells drew tears. Poets mirrored religious evils. Social reformers like Kandukuri Veeresalingam fought against such unjust practices, resulting in a ban on child marriages by the Sarada Act.

In the name of religion, girls were turned into prostitutes called Matangi and Murali in Maharashtra, Basivi in Karnataka, Bhogini and Devadasi in Andhra Pradesh, Mahari in Kerala, and Neti in Assam. Gifted by the parents' to the temple in their childhood, these girls were supposed to dedicate their lives in the service of god. Breaking into song and dance on the occasion of festivals in temples and funeral processions of higher castes, they collected coins pelted at them by cheering crowds.

The prostitutes of those days were well versed in dance and music. The visitors were attracted to them by their proficiency in those arts. Rich and influential people vied with one another for the right of the first night. The customs have changed, but still the profession persists. A caste by the name of Devadasis (servants of God) was created and made permanent by the priestly class and the king's preceptors.

Jogins

Still the practice of Jogini, a remnant of Devadasi system, is prevalent in the Telangana area of Andhra Pradesh. These dalit girls, the lowest rung of the social ladder in India, are supposed to be wedded to god. Their sexual exploitation goes unabated in the garb of divine sanction.

The village priest known as Pothuraju tied the sacred thread to the Bhogini, the girl offered by parents, and formally declared she was married to god. He or the village landlord exploited her sexually first after she came of age. Later on, village officials and others with money, power, and influence enjoyed her. In the course of time, the girls turned into prostitutes and acquired a caste of their own. No one would marry Devadasis, Bhoginis, or Jogins since they were god's spouses. The girls did not enjoy any rights and their children had no social recognition. Their daughters became servants of god like them while their sons became orphans.

Some parents handed over their girls to temples. A girl belonging to higher castes was called Devadasi according to the Vaishnava tradition and that of a lower, untouchable caste, Bhogini or Jogini, according to the Saiva tradition.

Religion approved the system in the name of service to god.

Tonsuring of Children

In the name of fulfilling vows, small kids are taken to temples and tonsured. Children do not know what is happening to them. This religious practice is in vogue. Children are taught that by sacrificing their hair to god, they will fulfill their wishes and achieve whatever they want. It has become a very popular superstition.

Some parents take their children to Tirupati-Tirumala, the abode of Lord Venkateswara, for the ceremony. The ignorant and helpless children bow their heads. As colleagues make fun of their tonsured heads, the children shrink in despair. Such practices survive because parents regard children as their property. The United Nations wants parents to honor children's rights.

Recitation of "Venkateswara Suprabhatam" is a ritual in many homes. Devotees revel in the recitation, although they do not know the meaning of the verses in Sanskrit. When the author asked a Telugu gathering in New York if anyone understood the meaning of "Suprabhatam," many blinked. "Suprabhatam" contains sex and obscenities, which should be out of bounds for children. The pity is that parents themselves do not know its meaning.

Clad in black, devotees trek their way to a temple atop Sabarimalai hill in Kerala. They are thrilled when a light is sighted enveloping the hill on a particular day every year. Although it has been revealed that god does not cast the "sacred" light but instead it is the result of tons of camphor burnt by the Kerala Electricity Board, devotees continue to throng the place. Parents make their children follow in their footsteps literally and figuratively. Parents are thus thrusting their customs, traditions, and blind beliefs on children. If children really understood the origins of Ayyappa, they would be revolted.

Parents should realize that they would not make their children devoted or disciplined by making them recite "Venkateswara Suprabhatam" (Invocation to Lord Venkateswara in the early morning). The Suprabhatam is a verse recited to wake up Lord Venkateswara, who is sleeping and fatigued after the previous night's love play with his consort, Lakshmi. So long as children recite it in Sanskrit without understanding its meaning there is no trouble. But what if they were to understand its meaning? Then parents would not force them to learn it. Similarly, in the devotional songs of Tyagaraja and Kshetrayya (devotee poets of South India) and in Pothana's (the Telugu poet in the middle centuries in South India) Bhagavatha, there are repulsive references to sex.

Many Hindu scriptures contain matters that should not be taught to children. Take the Bhagavad Gita, for instance. It says that women and "sudras" come out of sinful vagina. Srikrishna glorifies violence and incites Arjuna to indulge in killing.

Krishna is a god incarnation of Hindus who proclaimed through his holy scripture, Gita, that he created the four-caste system. He is guide to Arjun, who followed his instructions and killed his own kith and kin. Krishna justified the killings in the name of karma or fate, saying that the past life decided the nature of the killings and hence there is nothing wrong in killing people. The influence of Gita and the killings it has inspired is very popular in India.

The fatalistic theory of the "Gita" emasculates students. Everything in this birth is attributed to actions in the previous birth, implying that little can be done by anybody now. Should not such harmful material be deleted before it is taught? How can a holy book contain unholy matters?

Similarly, Manu's "Dharma Sastra" talks about caste-based judgments and punishments. Can it be taught today? Vastu Sastra too talks about caste culture with reference to its unscientific postulations.

JEWS

Jews continue to practice circumcision for male children, citing medical opinion in its favor. Innumerable instances of children undergoing hardships because of such a procedure have come to light. Many associations of Jews have also opposed it. Recently, the American Society of Pediatricians dubbed circumcision as unscientific.

Christopher Hitchens in *God Is Not Great* has some interesting points on circumcision among Jews:

> In other cultures, notably the "Judeo-Christian," it is the sexual mutilation of small boys that is insisted upon. (For some reason, little girls can be Jewish without genital alteration: it is useless to look for consistency in the covenants that people believe they have made with god). Here, the original motivation appears to be twofold. The shedding of blood—which is insisted upon at circumcision ceremonies—is most probably a symbolic survival from the animal and human sacrifices that were such a feature of the gore-soaked land-

scape of the Old Testament. By adhering to the pacific, parents could offer to sacrifice a part of the child as a stand-in for the whole. Objections to interference with something that god must have designed with care—the human penis—were overcome by the invented dogma that Adam was born circumcised and in the image of god. Indeed, it is argued by some rabbis that Moses, too, was born circumcised, though this claim may result from the fact that his own circumcision is nowhere mentioned in the Pentateuch.

The second purpose—very unambivalently stated by Maimonides—was the same as for girls: the destruction as far as possible of the pleasurable side of sexual intercourse. Here is what the sage tells us in his *Guide to the Perplexed*:

> With regard to circumcision, one of the reasons for it is, in my opinion, the wish to bring about a decrease in sexual intercourse and a weakening of the organ in question, so that this activity is diminished and the organ be in as quiet a state as possible. It has been though that circumcision perfects what is defective congenitally. . . . How can natural things be defective so that they need to be perfected from outside, all the more because *we know how useful the foreskin is for that member?* In fact this commandment has not been prescribed with a view to perfecting what is defective congenitally, but to perfecting what is defective morally. The bodily pain caused to that member is the real purpose of circumcision. . . . The fact that circumcision weakens that faculty of sexual excitement and sometimes perhaps diminished the pleasure is indubitable. For if at birth this member has been made to bleed and has had its covering taken away from it, it must indubitably be weakened.

BUDDHISTS

Buddhism is one of the biggest religions in the world. Although it was born in India, it flourished in China, Japan, Thailand, Myanmar, Sri

Lanka, Tibet, Malaysia, Indonesia, Korea, Vietnam, Laos, and other countries. It has only a token presence in the country of its origin.

The founder of Buddhism highlighted human values, ethics, and the quest for truth without bothering about god. Hindus in India successfully killed Buddhism by co-opting Buddha into their pantheon of gods as a reincarnation of Lord Vishnu. Buddha's followers split to have their own schools of thought like Hinayana, Mahayana, and Vajrayana. But all of them deified the Buddha. Statues, temples, ashrams, and lamas became part of the order. As in other religions, the followers fought among themselves and killed each other.

In Tibet, lamas are chosen even when they are children like the Shankaracharyas in India are. The present Dalai Lama is the fourteenth in the series. The thirteenth lama died in 1933. Lamas are regarded as a reincarnation of god. A lama is said be aware of his previous birth. There are legends of miracles happening when a lama is born.

Lama Dondan was a four-year-old boy of Tuxer, a small village in Tibet, living happily with his parents and playing with other children when he was picked as the fourteenth Dalai Lama. He was brought to Lhasa and declared Dalai Lama on February 22, 1939. Segregated from other children, he was taught religion in the Potola Palace and was declared a world Buddhist leader when he attained age fifteen. In 1950, the Dalai Lama was formally enthroned as a religious head. In his nineteenth year, the Dalai Lama visited China and sought recognition for his Buddhist leadership. The Communist leaders of China, however, turned down his plea. When the Chinese occupied Tibet in 1959, the Dalai Lama fled the mountainous country for his life and sought asylum in India. The government of India granted him asylum and helped him set up his base at Dharmashala. Since then, he has been touring the world preaching freedom and human rights. The Dalai Lama, who was given the Nobel Prize in 1989, continues to preach superstitions. He has yet to realize that he has no supernatural powers and his claims of previous births are mere lies.

The fifteenth Lama has already been chosen—he was six years old when he was appointed to the position. Ling Ringpoche is now undergoing religious training at Dharmashala. The lamas are kept in "religious prisons" away from society and scientific education.

In the Buddhist country of Bhutan, nestling in the Himalayan hills, rulers insulated people from the outside world by denying them the means of communication. That television could not make its advent in Bhutan until 1999 was a telling commentary on the cruelty of religion. Even in Tibet, the Buddhist lamas were guilty of despotism for a long period. Even as they talked of dharma, ethics, and compassion, they controlled the population tightly.

What should be the plan to prevent child abuse?

Children should be brought up without allowing religion to influence them. If they are steeped in religion attributed to them as a hereditary feature, they can not get out of it.

Religion rests on belief and trust.

Only those who got out of religion have contributed to progress and development in all ages.

Charles Darwin started his career as Christian believer in creation and gradually changed toward the theory of evolution due to the accumulation of evidence and facts. The theory of evolution goes against the Bible, but Charles Darwin stuck to his position due to verifiable facts. It upset all those who were believers in the Creation story.

The urges to learn new things, to study, research, and live in tune with nature are all above religion.

Religion treats everything as God's creation and asks its followers to believe in it. It implies that there is little that man can discover or invent and progress. New things have, however, come to light because of the inborn quest to learn new things and the urge to question. Those who peeped out of religion could become leaders of society.

It takes twenty years for the brain of a child to mature to its full capacity. Adherence to religion, however, thwarts brain development. Parents, priests, and other social leaders teach children blind beliefs and inculcate in them fear and devotion, all of which kill their inquisitiveness. The brain that should blossom as years roll by is instead blunted. Religion has no regrets, because a thinking soul is a threat to religion.

We should take care of children, listen to them, answer their queries, and encourage their inquisitiveness. Children should not be bossed, beaten, or threatened. They should not be prevented from asking questions, however inconvenient they might be. It is a crime to warn children that they will lose sight or fall ill if they do not worship God or raise unpalatable questions.

Sex, politics, and religion coming under the purview of elders should not be imposed on children. Children should have the freedom to choose any religion once they attain eighteen years of age and are mature enough to know what they are doing.

Religion should be taught on scientific lines in schools. Then children will have an opportunity to question and get their doubts clarified and evince interest in the subject.

Children should not inherit religion. If parents belong to one political party, it should not be taken for granted that their children belong to that party. A similar logic should be applied with respect to religion.

Children should be insulated from religious hatred and intolerance. They should not be threatened in the name of gods, devils, demons, apparitions, or other invisible entities of power. They need ethics devoid of fear. They should be taught that societies progress when their members are upright in conduct and cooperate with each other. They should be educated on the role of science in development. Superstitions should not be taught under any circumstances.

Parents should be educated about the United Nation's Charter for Children. Honoring children's rights does not mean separating children from parents. Parents should be told of injustices unwittingly meted out to children so that they mend their ways.

CHILDREN'S INQUISITIVENESS

Children, irrespective of their place of birth, color, or race, are curious and inquisitive. They have no inhibitions or fear. They want to question and learn about everything. But unable to answer their children, parents snub them and instill into them fear and blind devotion. Threats and fear kill their curiosity. For instance, parents never answer the children's question as to how birth takes place. Children get confused as they hear many conflicting answers.

Teaching children that the god who created human beings fulfills desires or forgives sins and crimes if he is worshipped or propitiated is a crime. Such teachings sap children's initiative to excel in life.

All religions are opposed to human values. The very assertion that we live for God is contrary to human values. Children should be rescued from religion and restored to humanity.

THE ROAD MAP FOR THE NEW MILLENNIUM

Children should be educated on the need for morals, upright conduct, and mutual cooperation, and should be instructed that violence is bad. Understanding and questioning are natural human urges. They should be told that gods and demons, devils and apparitions, and heaven and hell are all man's creations, and that the Vedas, Upanishads, Bhagavad Gita, Bible, Koran, and Zend-Avesta are all human works. We should ensure that children take the contents as mere stories. They should be told that life is supreme, that it should be respected, and that the idea of life being miserable or bad is meaningless.

Parents should realize that religion should not be ascribed to children as a hereditary trait. Children should be kept away from religion, just as they are kept from prostitution, politics, obscenity, and marriage. Taking children to temples, tonsuring their heads to fulfill vows, encouraging blind worship, and terrorizing them in the name of God are all unwarranted.

One hundred and ninety-one countries have signed the Children's Charter and their parliaments have begun to adopt legislation to implement the charter. Parents have to appreciate and accept that children have some inherent rights. In schools, children should be educated about their rights. Radio, television, and newspapers should carry on a publicity campaign on children's rights.

The priestly class will attempt to oppose children's rights. If priests lose their grip over religion, they lose their livelihood. Society should take cognizance of such a threat and move forward.

The Children's Charter is yet to be adopted by a developed country like the United States because of opposition from religious figures. Even parents hesitate to support it, fearing the loosening of their grip over children. Recognition of children's rights is in the interest of their future. Children, who move about freely without fear, learn everything, behave morally, and in cooperation with others will contribute to society's development.

Parents should realize that they are not inculcating discipline but only fear by promoting God's worship. They are stifling their innate curiosity.

Parents might have been brought up that way. But they should not impose their religious customs, habits, superstitions, and devotion on their children and leave them as a legacy. They should break with the unhealthy past at least in the new millennium.

ROLE OF CULTS IN CHILD ABUSE BY RELIGIONS

What is the role of cults in child abuse? Several cults are functioning worldwide. Here is a sample list:

Ananda Marga
Anatmananda

Aum Shin Rikyo
Baha'i
Children of God
Emissaries of Divine Light
Falun Gong
Garbage Eaters
Hare Krishna
Heaven's Gate
Jehovah's Witnesses
Jim Jones
Mormons
Nigerian Student Cults
People's Temple
Bhagavan Sri Sathya Sai Baba
Siddha Yoga
Solar Temple
Televangelists
Transcendental Meditation

Cults are very dangerous and harmful to children.

Children not only suffer, but sometimes die in cult practices.

For example, allegations of child abuse in the House of Judah, an ultrafundamentalist Michigan sect, resulted in the removal of sixty-two children from a camp run by the sect.[11] This action was prompted by the death of a twelve-year-old boy who was beaten to death for refusing to do his chores. A 1983 report by Ray E. Heifer, MD, of the Department of Pediatrics/Human Development of Michigan State University, stated: "These nutritionally healthy bodies have been moderately to severely injured by repetitive beatings and other physical insults. Of the first 50–55 children examined by a physician after John's death a full 20% had signs of severe physical abuse. For the children greater than five years of age this percentage increases to approximately 40% and for boys in this age range, the figure is 70–75%. Thus, the likelihood of a male child reaching adolescence without showing physical signs of severe physical abuse to his body is less than 25%.[11]

House of Judah leader William A. Lewis was convicted, along with seven other members of the group, for enslaving children and holding twelve-year-old John Yarbough in involuntary servitude until he was beaten to death in 1983.[12]

Lewis is now out of jail and has created a new community of seventy people in rural Alabama.[13]

In 1986, fifteen members of the Yahweh Temple of the Black Hebrew Israelites were charged with ritualistic beatings and child torture. Five children who were placed under protective custody by authorities told how they were hit with switches, rods, and other items in bizarre ritualistic beatings.[14]

The Swiss periodical *Sonntagsblick* told of twenty uneducated Children of God youngsters living isolated from other people in a house due to be demolished in a rural Zurich parish. There had been claims that sect girls were sometimes driven across the border to Germany to go on the street. A Bern children's news agency reported the case of a twelve-year-old girl from the group who was admitted to a hospital suffering severely from venereal disease. The child was said to be in a pitiable state, quite apathetic, and barely able to read or write.[15]

Children raised in cults have little knowledge about the world, especially if their group is isolated. Therefore, when they leave a cult, even if its practices and beliefs were highly deviant, they will take the cult's worldview with them because they know no other. Hence, their capacity to think critically and act independently may be deficient, not merely "blocked" as may be the case with ex-cultists. Ironically, those children who were most uncooperative in the cult—those who rebelled—may be most likely to make an effective transition into mainstream society because they will not have imbibed the group's worldview so completely as others. The abuses to which children have been subjected can be horrendous. The degree to which cult leaders can escape accountability by hiding behind the First Amendment is troubling in the United States and in other countries like India, where the government is lukewarm toward the cult gurus. There are several complaints against cult Guru Sai Baba of Andhra Pradesh regarding pedophilia, and these complaints led to the cancellation of educational world conferences too. No organization less than UNESCO, consulate of the United States, made complaints about sexual abuses of Sai Baba and warned youth not to visit the religious hermit of Sai Baba in Puttaparthi, Andhra Pradesh, India. Yet the governments in India never booked a case nor inquired into allegations despite the agitations by humanist organizations. The lack of concern and action about this problem is shameful.

1. A destructive cult tends to be totalitarian in its control of its members' behavior. Cults are likely to dictate in great detail not only what members believe; but also what members wear and eat, when and where members work, sleep, and bathe, and how members think, speak, and conduct familial, marital, or sexual relationships.

2. A destructive cult tends to have an ethical double standard. Members are urged to be obedient to the cult and to carefully follow cult rules. They are also encouraged to be revealing and open in the group, confessing all to the leaders. On the other hand, outside the group they are encouraged to act unethically, manipulating outsiders or nonmembers, either by deceiving or simply revealing very little about themselves or the group. In contrast to destructive cults, honorable groups teach members to abide by one set of ethics and act ethically and truthfully to all people in all situations.

3. A destructive cult has only two basic purposes: recruiting new members and fund-raising. Altruistic movements, established religions, and other honorable groups also recruit and raise funds. However, these actions are incidental to an honorable group's main purpose of improving the lives of its members and of humankind in general. Destructive cults may claim to make social contributions, but in actuality such claims are

superficial and only serve as gestures or fronts for recruiting and fund-raising. A cult's real goal is to increase the prestige and often the wealth of the leader.

4. A destructive cult appears to be innovative and exclusive. The leader claims to be breaking with tradition, offering something novel, and instituting the ONLY viable system for change that will solve life's problems or the world's ills. But these claims are empty and only used to recruit members who are then surreptitiously subjected to mind control to inhibit their ability to examine the actual validity of the claims of the leader and the cult.

5. A destructive cult is authoritarian in its power structure. The leader is regarded as the supreme authority. He or she may delegate certain power to a few subordinates for the purpose of seeing that members adhere to the leader's wishes. There is no appeal outside his or her system to a greater system of justice. For example, if a school teacher feels unjustly treated by a principal, an appeal can be made to the superintendent. In a destructive cult, the leader claims to have the only and final ruling on all matters.

6. A destructive cult's leader is a self-appointed messianic person claiming to have a special mission in life. For example, leaders of flying saucer cults claim that beings from outer space have commissioned them to lead people away from Earth, so that only the leaders can save them from impending doom.

7. A destructive cult's leader centers the veneration of members upon himself or herself. Priests, rabbis, ministers, democratic leaders, and other leaders of genuinely altruistic movements focus the veneration of adherents on God or a set of ethical principles. Cult leaders, in contrast, keep the focus of love, devotion, and allegiance on themselves.

8. A destructive cult's leader tends to be determined, domineering, and charismatic. Such a leader effectively persuades followers to abandon or alter their families, friends, and careers to follow the cult. The leader then takes control over followers' possessions, money, time, and lives.

BIBLIOGRAPHY

Ali, Ayaan Hirsi. *Infidel.* New York: Free Press, 2008.

American Academy of Pediatrics. "Religious Exemptions from Child Abuse Statutes." *Pediatrics* 99 (February 1997): 279–81.

Asser, Seth, and Rita Swan. "Child Fatalities from Religion Motivated Medical Neglect." *Pediatrics* 101 (April 1998): 625–29.

Barrett, Stephen. *The New Health Robbers.* Philadelphia: George Stickney, 1981.

Basu, Rekha. "Whatever Your Religion, Children Deserve Medical Care." *Des Moines Register,* February 17, 2006, 9A.

Battin, Margaret. *Ethics in the Sanctuary: Examining the Practices of Organized Religion.* New Haven, CT: Yale University Press, 1990.

Bedi, Rahul. "Schoolboy Recruit who Killed 28 in First Operation." *Telegraph* (Kolkata), September 22, 2002.

Bergman, Jerry. *Blood Transfusions: A History and Evaluation of the Religious, Biblical, and Medical Objections.* Clayton, CA: Witness Inc., 1994.

———. *Jehovah's Witnesses: A Comprehensive and Selectively Annotated Bibliography.* Westport, CT: Greenwood Press, 1999.

Bottoms, Bette, et al. "In the Name of God: A Profile of Religion-Related Child Abuse." *Journal of Social Issues* 51 (1995): 85–111.

Brenneman, Richard. *Deadly Blessings: Faith Healing on Trial.* Amherst, NY: Prometheus Books, 1990.

Burns, John F. "Palestinian Summer Camp Offers the Games of War." *New York Times,* August 3, 2000.

Cass, Ramona. "We Let Our Son Die." *Journal of Christian Nursing* (Spring 1987): 4–8.

Chatterjee, Aroup. *The Final Verdict.* Kolkata, India: Meteor Books, 2003.

Coalition to Repeal Exemptions to Child Abuse Laws. "Death by Religious Exemption." Boston: Massachusetts Community for Children and Youth, 1991.

Damore, Leo. *The Crime of Dorothy Sheridan.* New York: Dell, 1992.

Dawkins, Richard. *The God Delusion.* New York: Bantam Books, 2006.

Dorf, Matthew. "Palestinian Children's Show Sparks Anger in Washington." Jewish Telegraph Agency. New York, August 17, 1998.

Dudkevitch, Margot. "Fatah Tries to Use 11 Year-Old Boy as Human Bomb." *Jerusalem Post*, March 16, 2004.

Dwyer, James. "Spiritual Treatment Exemptions to Child Medical Neglect Laws: What We Outsiders Should Think." *Notre Dame Law Review* 76 (2000): 147–77.

Erlanger, Steven. "Suicide Blast Kills 4 at Tel Aviv Market: 16 Year-Old Bomber Injures 32 Others at Outdoor Stalls." *San Francisco Chronicle*, November 2, 2004.

Fletcher, Marion. "Palestinian Propaganda Encouraging Children to Join Fight Against Israel." *NBC News Transcripts*, May 8, 2001.

Fox, Robin. *Lancet*, September 17, 1994

Fraser, Caroline. *God's Perfect Child: Living and Dying in the Christian Science Church*. New York: Holt Metropolitan Books, 1999.

———. "Suffering Children and the Christian Science Church." *Atlantic Monthly*, April 1995, 105–20.

Gifford, Bill. "A Matter of Faith." *Philadelphia Magazine*, September 1997, 96–101, 154–56.

Godbole, Shreeran. "Flood of Foreign Funds in India." http://www.hvk .org/articles/0204/27.html (accessed September 3, 2008).

Hamilton, Marci. *God vs. the Gavel: Religion and the Rule of Law*. Boston: Cambridge University Press, 2005.

Ha'aretz Staff and Agencies (Tel Aviv). "16 Year-Old Rishon Bomber Was Youngest to Strike in Israel." June 9, 2002.

Harel, Amos. "Palestinians: Policeman Hurt in IDF Raid in Gaza Refugee Camp." *Ha'aretz*, March 25, 2004.

Harris, Sam. *The End of Faith: Religion, Terror and the Future of Reason*. New York: W. W. Norton, 2004.

———. *Letter to a Christian Nation*. New York: Alfred A. Knopf, 2006.

"Hebrew Israelites Charged with Abuse." *Cult Observer*, May/June 1986, p. 28

Hitchens, Christopher. "Childhood's End." *Vanity Fair*, January 2006.

———. *God is Not Great: How Religion Poisons Everything*. New York: Hachette Books Group, 2007.

"House of Judah Leader and Members Sentenced." *Cult Observer.* March/April 1987, p. 11.

Itamar, Marcus. "Arafat Tells Young Children to be *Shahids.*" Palestinian Media Watch *Bulletin*, August 21, 2002.

Johnson, Reed. "Prophet & Loss." *Detroit News*, March 9, 1991, pp. 3C, 4C.

Kase, Lori. "Profile: Rita Swan." *American Health* (July/August 1992): 16, 18–19.

Kaunitz, A. M., C. Spence, T. S. Danielson, R. W. Rochat, D. A. Grimes, "Perinatal and Maternal Mortality in a Religious Group Avoiding Obstetrical Care." *American Journal of Obstetrics and Gynecology* 150 (December 1, 1984): 826–31.

Kohn, Alfie. "Mind over Matter." *New England Monthly* (March 1988): 58–63, 96.

Kramer, Linda. *The Religion That Kills: Christian Science, Abuse, Neglect, and Mind Control.* Lafayette, LA: Huntington House, 1999.

Larabee, Mark. "Church Controls All, Ex-Follower Says." *Oregonian*, April 26, 1998, p. 1.

———. "The Faith Healers." *Oregonian*, November 29, 1988, p. 1. Several articles by Larabee appear in the November 30 and December 1, 1998, issues of *Oregonian*.

Larabee, Mark, and Peter Sleeth. "Faith Healing Raises Questions of Law's Duty—Belief or Life?" *Oregonian*. June 7, 1998, p. 1.

Marcus, Itamar. "Palestinian Authority Renews Efforts to Have Palestinian Children Die in Confrontations." *Palestinian Media Watch Bulletin*, October 1, 2002.

Margolick, David. "Death and Faith, Law and Christian Science." *New York Times*, August 6, 1990, sec. 1.

Marquand, Robert. "New Faces Join Fray in Kashmir." *Christian Science Monitor*, May 2, 2000.

Massachusetts Committee for Children and Youth. "Death by Religious Exemption: An Advocacy Report on the Need to Repeal Religious Exemptions to Necessary Medical Care for Children." Boston: Massachusetts Committee for Children and Youth, 1992.

———. "Jeopardizing Children's Lives: A Policy Report on the Need for the U. S. Dept. of Health and Human Services to Require Repeal of Religious Exemptions to Medical Care for Children." Boston: Massachusetts Committee for Children and Youth, 1994.

Massie, Ann. "The Religion Clauses and Parental Health Care Decision

Making for Children: Suggestions for a New Approach." *Hastings Constitutional Law Quarterly* 21 (1994): 725–75.

McLaughlin, Margaret. "This Too Is Child Abuse: Medical Treatment Denied for Religious Reasons." *Counseling Interviewer* (Fall 1990): 19–20.

"Michigan Cult Leader's New Settlement." *Cult Observer* 8, no. 4, p. 3.

Murdock, Rosamond. *Suffer the Children*. Santa Fe: Health Press, 1992.

Nasrin, Taslima. *My Girlhood: An Autobiography*. Kali for Women, 2001.

"PA Mufti of Jerusalem and Palestine Discuss the *Intifada*." Middle East Media Research Institute, November 8, 2000. http://www.memri.org/.

Park, Robert. *Voodoo Science: The Road from Foolishness to Fraud*. New York: Oxford University Press, 2000.

Parker, Larry. *We Let Our Son Die*. Irvine, CA: Harvest House, 1980.

Rajaram, N. S. "Meltdown in Pakistan." *The Voice of Dharma*. www.voi.org/books/cpak/ch1.html

Randi, James. *The Faith Healers*. Amherst, NY: Prometheus Books, 1987.

Reid Weiner, Justus. "The Recruitment of Children in Current Palestinian Strategy." *Jerusalem Issue Brief*, October 1, 2002.

Schechter, Erik. "Two Palestinian Youths Shot Dead by the IDF." *Jerusalem Post,* March 25, 2003.

Schoepflin, Rennie. *Christian Science on Trial: Religious Healing in America*. Baltimore: Johns Hopkins University Press, 2003.

"Seek Death—The Life Will Be Given To You." *Palestinian Media Watch*. http://www.pmw.org.il.

"Seven Sect Members Get Prison Terms." *Minneapolis Star and Tribune*. December 20, 1986.

Shepard, Suzanne. "Suffer the Little Children." *Redbook*, October 1994, 68–72.

Shragai, Nadav. "Child writes to Mother, 'Rejoice over My Death.'" *Ha'aretz*, January 8, 2003.

Simmons, Thomas. *The Unseen Shore: Memories of a Christian Science Childhood*. Boston: Beacon, 1991.

Simpson, William. "Comparative Longevity in a College Cohort of Christian Scientists." *JAMA* 262 (September 22–29, 1989): 1657–58.

———. "Comparative Mortality of Two College Groups, 1945–83." *Mortality and Morbidity Weekly Report* 40 (August 23, 1991): 579–82.

"Sixty-Two Youths Taken Away from Religious Camp." *New York Times,* July 9, 1983.

Skolnick, Andrew. "Christian Scientists Claim Healing Efficacy Equal If Not Superior to That of Medicine." *JAMA* 264 (September 19, 1990): 1379–81.

———. "Faith Healers: How Charismatic 'Healers' Promise Miracles while Picking the Public's Pocket." *Social Issues and Healthcare Review* (Spring 1988): 46–52.

———. "Religious Exemptions to Child Neglect Laws Still Being Passed Despite Convictions of Parents." *JAMA* 264 (September 12, 1990): 1226, 1229, 1233.

Stern, Jessica. "Pakistan's Jihad Culture." *Foreign Affairs*, November/December 2000.

Stern, Jessica. "Meeting With the Muj." *Bulletin of the Atomic Scientists* 57, no. 1, pp. 42–50. http://www.thebulletin.org/article.php?art_ofn=jf01stern.

Swami, Praveen. "Jehadi Groups Step Up Recruitment of Children." *The Hindu* (Chennai), September 9, 2003.

Swan, Rita. "Children, Medicine, Religion, and the Law." *Advances in Pediatrics* 44 (1997): 491–543.

———. "Christian Science, Faith Healing, and the Law." *Free Inquiry* (Spring 1984): 4–9.

———. "Discrimination de Jure: Religious Exemptions for Medical Neglect." *APSAC Advisor* 7 (Winter 1994): 35–38.

———. "Faith Healing, Christian Science, and the Medical Care of Children." *New England Journal of Medicine* 309 (December 29, 1983): 1639–41.

———. "First Amendment Does Not Give the Right to Injure Children." *Los Angeles Times*, July 14, 1990, F16.

———. "Fragile Life: Religious Beliefs That Kill Children." *Kentucky Hospitals* (Winter 1989): 8–12.

———. "The Law Should Protect All Children." *Journal of Christian Nursing* (Spring 1987): 40.

"Switzerland." *Cult Observer* 8, no. 4, p. 9.

Warraq, Ib, ed. *Leaving Islam*. Amherst, NY: Prometheus Books, 2003.

———. *Why I Am Not a Muslim*. Amherst, NY: Prometheus Books, 1995.

PART II

CHARTER OF RIGHTS OF CHILDREN

The Convention on the Rights of the Child was adopted and opened for signature, ratification, and accession by General Assembly resolution 44/25 of 20 November 1989. It entered into force 2 September 1990, in accordance with article 49.

The States Parties to the present Convention,

Considering that, in accordance with the principles proclaimed in the Charter of the United Nations, recognition of the inherent dignity and of the equal and inalienable rights of all members of the human family is the foundation of freedom, justice, and peace in the world,

Bearing in mind that the peoples of the United Nations have, in the Charter, reaffirmed their faith in fundamental human rights and in the dignity and worth of the human person and have determined to promote social progress and better standards of life in larger freedom,

Recognizing that the United Nations has, in the Universal Declaration of Human Rights and in the International Covenants on Human Rights, proclaimed and agreed that everyone is entitled to all the rights and freedoms set forth therein, without distinction of any kind, such as race, color, sex, language, religion, political or other opinion, national or social origin, property, birth or other status,

Recalling that, in the Universal Declaration of Human Rights, the United Nations has proclaimed that childhood is entitled to special care and assistance,

Convinced that the family, as the fundamental group of society and the natural environment for the growth and well-being of all its members and particularly children, should be afforded the necessary protection and assistance so that it can fully assume its responsibilities within the community,

Recognizing that the child, for the full and harmonious development of his or her personality, should grow up in a family environment, in an atmosphere of happiness, love and understanding,

Considering that the child should be fully prepared to live an individual life in society and brought up in the spirit of the ideals proclaimed in the Charter of the United Nations and in particular in the spirit of peace, dignity, tolerance, freedom, equality and solidarity,

Bearing in mind that the need to extend particular care to the child has been stated in the Geneva Declaration of the Rights of the Child of 1924 and in the Declaration of the Rights of the Child adopted by the General Assembly on 20 November 1959 and recognized in the Universal Declaration of Human Rights, in the International Covenant on Civil and Political Rights (in particular in articles 23 and 24), in the International Covenant on Economic, Social, and Cultural Rights (in particular in article 10) and in the statutes and relevant instruments of specialized agencies and international organizations concerned with the welfare of children,

Bearing in mind that, as indicated in the Declaration of the Rights of the Child, the child, by reason of his physical and mental immaturity, needs special safeguards and care, including appropriate legal protection, before as well as after birth,

Recalling the provisions of the Declaration on Social and Legal Principles relating to the Protection and Welfare of Children, with Special Reference to Foster Placement and Adoption Nationally and Internationally; the United Nations Standard Minimum Rules for the Administration of Juvenile Justice (The Beijing Rules); and the Declaration on the Protection of Women and Children in Emergency and Armed Conflict,

Recognizing that, in all countries in the world, there are children living in exceptionally difficult conditions and that such children need special consideration,

Taking due account of the importance of the traditions and cultural values of each people for the protection and harmonious development of the child,

Recognizing the importance of international cooperation for improving the living conditions of children in every country, in particular in the developing countries,

Have agreed as follows:

Article 1

For the purposes of the present Convention, a child means every human being below the age of eighteen years unless under the law applicable to the child, majority is attained earlier.

Article 2

States Parties shall respect and ensure the rights set forth in the present Convention to each child within their jurisdiction without discrimination of any kind, irrespective of the child's or his or her parent's or legal guardian's race, color, sex, language, religion, political or other opinion, national, ethnic or social origin, property, disability, birth or other status.

States Parties shall take all appropriate measures to ensure that the child is protected against all forms of discrimination or punishment on the basis of the status, activities, expressed opinions, or beliefs of the child's parents, legal guardians, or family members.

Article 3

In all actions concerning children, whether undertaken by public or private social welfare institutions, courts of law, administrative authorities or legislative bodies, the best interests of the child shall be a primary consideration.

States Parties undertake to ensure the child such protection and care as is necessary for his or her well-being, taking into account the rights and duties of his or her parents, legal guardians, or other individuals legally responsible for him or her, and, to this end, shall take all appropriate legislative and administrative measures.

States Parties shall ensure that the institutions, services and facilities responsible for the care or protection of children shall conform with the standards established by competent authorities, particularly in the areas of safety, health, in the number and suitability of their staff, as well as competent supervision.

Article 4

States Parties shall undertake all appropriate legislative, administrative and other measures for the implementation of the rights recognized in the present Convention. With regard to economic, social, and cultural rights, States Parties shall undertake such measures to the maximum extent of their available resources and, where needed, within the framework of international cooperation.

Article 5

States Parties shall respect the responsibilities, rights and duties of parents or, where applicable, the members of the extended family or community as provided for by local custom, legal guardians or other persons legally responsible for the child, to provide, in a manner consistent with the evolving capacities of the child, appropriate direction and guidance in the exercise by the child of the rights recognized in the present Convention.

Article 6

States Parties recognize that every child has the inherent right to life.

States Parties shall ensure to the maximum extent possible the survival and development of the child.

Article 7

The child shall be registered immediately after birth and shall have the right from birth to a name, the right to acquire a nationality and, as far as possible, the right to know and be cared for by his or her parents.

States Parties shall ensure the implementation of these rights in accordance with their national law and their obligations under the relevant international instruments in this field, in particular where the child would otherwise be stateless.

Article 8

States Parties undertake to respect the right of the child to preserve his or her identity, including nationality, name and family relations as recognized by law without unlawful interference.

Where a child is illegally deprived of some or all of the elements of his or her identity, States Parties shall provide appropriate assistance and protection, with a view to reestablishing speedily his or her identity.

Article 9

States Parties shall ensure that a child shall not be separated from his or her parents against their will, except when competent authorities subject to judicial review determine, in accordance with applicable law and procedures, that such separation is necessary for the best interests of the child. Such determination may be necessary in a particular case such as one involving abuse or neglect of the child by the parents, or one where the parents are living separately and a decision must be made as to the child's place of residence.

In any proceedings pursuant to paragraph 1 of the present article, all interested parties shall be given an opportunity to participate in the proceedings and make their views known.

States Parties shall respect the right of the child who is separated from one or both parents to maintain personal relations and direct contact with both parents on a regular basis, except if it is contrary to the child's best interests.

Where such separation results from any action initiated by a State Party, such as the detention, imprisonment, exile, deportation or death (including death arising from any cause while the person is in the custody of the State) of one or both parents or of the child, that State Party shall, upon request, provide the parents, the child or, if appropriate, another member of the family with the essential information concerning the whereabouts of the absent member(s) of the family unless the provision of the information would be detrimental to the well-being of the child. States Parties shall further ensure that the submission of such a request shall of itself entail no adverse consequences for the person(s) concerned.

Article 10

In accordance with the obligation of States Parties under article 9, paragraph 1, applications by a child or his or her parents to enter or leave a State Party for the purpose of family reunification shall be dealt with by States Parties in a positive, humane, and expeditious manner. States Parties shall further ensure that the submission of such a request shall entail no adverse consequences for the applicants and for the members of their family.

A child whose parents reside in different States shall have the right to maintain on a regular basis, save in exceptional circumstances personal relations and direct contacts with both parents. Towards that end and in accordance with the obligation of States Parties under article 9, paragraph 1, States Parties shall respect the right of the child and his or her parents to leave any country, including their own and to enter their own country. The right to leave any country shall be subject only to such restrictions as are prescribed by law and which are necessary to protect the national security, public order (order public), public health or morals or the rights and freedoms of others and are consistent with the other rights recognized in the present Convention.

Article 11

States Parties shall take measures to combat the illicit transfer and nonreturn of children abroad.

To this end, States Parties shall promote the conclusion of bilateral or multilateral agreements or accession to existing agreements.

Article 12

States Parties shall assure to the child who is capable of forming his or her own views the right to express those views freely in all matters affecting the child, the views of the child being given due weight in accordance with the age and maturity of the child.

For this purpose, the child shall in particular be provided the opportunity to be heard in any judicial and administrative proceedings affecting the child, either directly, or through a representative or an appropriate body, in a manner consistent with the procedural rules of national law.

Article 13

The child shall have the right to freedom of expression; this right shall include freedom to seek, receive and impart information and ideas of all kinds, regardless of frontiers, either orally, in writing or in print, in the form of art, or through any other media of the child's choice.

The exercise of this right may be subject to certain restrictions, but these shall only be such as are provided by law and are necessary:

For respect of the rights or reputations of others; or

For the protection of national security or of public order (ordre public), or of public health or morals.

Article 14

States Parties shall respect the right of the child to freedom of thought, conscience and religion.

States Parties shall respect the rights and duties of the parents and, when applicable, legal guardians, to provide direction to the child in the exercise of his or her right in a manner consistent with the evolving capacities of the child.

Freedom to manifest one's religion or beliefs may be subject only to such limitations as are prescribed by law and are necessary to protect public safety, order, health or morals, or the fundamental rights and freedoms of others.

Article 15

States Parties recognize the rights of the child to freedom of association and to freedom of peaceful assembly.

No restrictions may be placed on the exercise of these rights other than those imposed in conformity with the law and which are necessary in a democratic society in the interests of national security or public safety, public order (ordre public), the protection of public health or morals or the protection of the rights and freedoms of others.

Article 16

No child shall be subjected to arbitrary or unlawful interference with his or her privacy, family, home or correspondence, nor to unlawful attacks on his or her honor and reputation.

The child has the right to the protection of the law against such interference or attacks.

Article 17

States Parties recognize the important function performed by the mass media and shall ensure that the child has access to information and material from a diversity of national and international sources, especially those aimed at the promotion of his or her social, spiritual, and moral well-being and physical and mental health. To this end, States Parties shall:

Encourage the mass media to disseminate information and material of social and cultural benefit to the child and in accordance with the spirit of article 29;

Encourage international cooperation in the production, exchange, and dissemination of such information and material from a diversity of cultural, national, and international sources;

Encourage the production and dissemination of children's books;

Encourage the mass media to have particular regard to the linguistic needs of the child who belongs to a minority group or who is indigenous;

Encourage the development of appropriate guidelines for the protection of the child from information and material injurious to his or her well-being, bearing in mind the provisions of articles 13 and 18.

Article 18

States Parties shall use their best efforts to ensure recognition of the principle that both parents have common responsibilities for the upbringing and development of the child. Parents or, as the case may be, legal guardians, have the primary responsibility for the upbringing and development of the child. The best interests of the child will be their basic concern.

For the purpose of guaranteeing and promoting the rights set forth in the present Convention, States Parties shall render appropriate assistance to parents and legal guardians in the performance of their childrearing responsibilities and shall ensure the development of institutions, facilities and services for the care of children.

States Parties shall take all appropriate measures to ensure that children of working parents have the right to benefit from childcare services and facilities for which they are eligible.

Article 19

States Parties shall take all appropriate legislative, administrative, social, and educational measures to protect the child from all forms of physical or mental violence, injury or abuse, neglect or negligent treatment, maltreatment or exploitation, including sexual abuse, while in the care of parent(s), legal guardian(s) or any other person who has the care of the child.

Such protective measures should, as appropriate, include effective procedures for the establishment of social programs to provide necessary support for the child and for those who have the care of the child, as well as for other forms of prevention and for identification, reporting, referral, investigation, treatment, and follow-up of instances of child maltreatment described heretofore, and, as appropriate, for judicial involvement.

Article 20

A child temporarily or permanently deprived of his or her family environment, or in whose own best interests cannot be allowed to remain in that environment, shall be entitled to special protection and assistance provided by the State.

States Parties shall in accordance with their national laws ensure alternative care for such a child.

Such care could include, inter alias, foster placement, kafalah of Islamic law, adoption or if necessary placement in suitable institutions for the care of children. When considering solutions, due regard shall be paid to the desirability of continuity in a child's upbringing and to the child's ethnic, religious, cultural, and linguistic background.

Article 21

States Parties that recognize and/or permit the system of adoption shall ensure that the best interests of the child shall be the paramount consideration and they shall:

Ensure that the adoption of a child is authorized only by competent authorities who determine, in accordance with applicable law and procedures and on the basis of all pertinent and reliable information, that the adoption is permissible in view of the child's status concerning parents, relatives and legal guardians and that, if required, the persons concerned have given their informed consent to the adoption on the basis of such counseling as may be necessary;

Recognize that intercountry adoption may be considered as an alternative means of child's care, if the child cannot be placed in a foster or an adoptive family or cannot in any suitable manner be cared for in the child's country of origin;

Ensure that the child concerned by intercountry adoption enjoys safeguards and standards equivalent to those existing in the case of national adoption;

Take all appropriate measures to ensure that, in intercountry adoption, the placement does not result in improper financial gain for those involved in it;

Promote, where appropriate, the objectives of the present article by concluding bilateral or multilateral arrangements or agreements and endeavor, within this framework, to ensure that the placement of the child in another country is carried out by competent authorities or organs.

Article 22

States Parties shall take appropriate measures to ensure that a child who is seeking refugee status or who is considered a refugee in accordance with applicable international or domestic law and procedures shall, whether unaccompanied or accompanied by his or her parents or by any other person, receive appropriate protection and humanitarian assistance in the enjoyment of applicable rights set forth in the present Convention and in other international human rights or humanitarian instruments to which the said States are Parties.

For this purpose, States Parties shall provide, as they consider appropriate, cooperation in any efforts by the United Nations and other competent intergovernmental organizations or nongovernmental organizations cooperating with the United Nations to protect and assist such a child and to trace the parents or other members of the family of any refugee child in order to obtain information necessary for reunification with his or her family. In cases where no parents or other members of the family can be found, the child shall be accorded the same protection as any other child permanently or temporarily deprived of his or her family environment for any reason, as set forth in the present Convention.

Article 23

States Parties recognize that a mentally or physically disabled child should enjoy a full and decent life, in conditions which ensure dignity, promote self-reliance, and facilitate the child's active participation in the community.

States Parties recognize the right of the disabled child to special care and shall encourage and ensure the extension, subject to available resources, to the eligible child and those responsible for his or her care, of assistance for which application is made and which is appropriate to the child's condition and to the circumstances of the parents or others caring for the child.

Recognizing the special needs of a disabled child, assistance extended in accordance with paragraph 2 of the present article shall be provided free of charge, whenever possible, taking into account the financial resources of the parents or others caring for the child and shall be designed to ensure that the disabled child has effective access to and receives education, training, healthcare services, rehabilitation services, preparation for employment and recreation opportunities in a manner conducive to the child's achieving the fullest possible social integration and individual development, including his or her cultural and spiritual development.

States Parties shall promote, in the spirit of international cooperation, the exchange of appropriate information in the field of preventive healthcare and of medical, psychological, and functional treatment of disabled children, including dissemination of and access to information concerning methods of rehabilitation, education and vocational services, with the aim of enabling States Parties to improve their capabilities and skills and to widen their experience in these areas. In this regard, particular account shall be taken of the needs of developing countries.

Article 24

States Parties recognize the right of the child to the enjoyment of the highest attainable standard of health and to facilities for the treatment of illness and rehabilitation of health. States Parties shall strive to ensure that no child is deprived of his or her right of access to such healthcare services.

States Parties shall pursue full implementation of this right and, in particular, shall take appropriate measures:

To diminish infant and child mortality;

To ensure the provision of necessary medical assistance and healthcare to all children with emphasis on the development of primary healthcare;

To combat disease and malnutrition, including within the framework of primary healthcare, through, inter alias, the application of readily available technology and through the provision of adequate nutritious foods and clean drinking water, taking into consideration the dangers and risks of environmental pollution;

To ensure appropriate prenatal and postnatal healthcare for mothers;

To ensure that all segments of society, in particular parents and children, are informed, have access to education and are supported in the use of basic knowledge of child health and nutrition, the advantages of breast-feeding, hygiene, and environmental sanitation and the prevention of accidents;

To develop preventive healthcare, guidance for parents and family planning education and services.

States Parties shall take all effective and appropriate measures with a view to abolishing traditional practices prejudicial to the health of children.

States Parties undertake to promote and encourage international cooperation with a view to achieving progressively the full realization of the right recognized in the present article. In this regard, particular account shall be taken of the needs of developing countries.

Article 25

States Parties recognize the right of a child who has been placed by the competent authorities for the purposes of care, protection or treatment of his or her physical or mental health, to a periodic review of the treatment provided to the child and all other circumstances relevant to his or her placement.

Article 26

States Parties shall recognize for every child the right to benefit from social security, including social insurance, and shall take the necessary measures to achieve the full realization of this right in accordance with their national law.

The benefits should, where appropriate, be granted, taking into account the resources and the circumstances of the child and persons having responsibility for the maintenance of the child, as well as any other consideration relevant to an application for benefits made by or on behalf of the child.

Article 27

States Parties recognize the right of every child to a standard of living adequate for the child's physical, mental, spiritual, moral, and social development.

The parent(s) or others responsible for the child have the primary responsibility to secure, within their abilities and financial capacities, the conditions of living necessary for the child's development.

States Parties, in accordance with national conditions and within their means, shall take appropriate measures to assist parents and others responsible for the child to implement this right and shall in case of need provide material assistance and support programs, particularly with regard to nutrition, clothing, and housing.

States Parties shall take all appropriate measures to secure the recovery of maintenance for the child from the parents or other persons having financial responsibility for the child, both within the State Party and from abroad. In particular, where the person having financial responsibility for the child lives in a State different from that of the child, States Parties shall promote the accession to international agreements or the conclusion of such agreements, as well as the making of other appropriate arrangements.

Article 28

States Parties recognize the right of the child to education and with a view to achieving this right progressively and on the basis of equal opportunity, they shall, in particular:

Make primary education compulsory and available free to all;

Encourage the development of different forms of secondary education, including general and vocational education, make them available and accessible to every child and take appropriate measures such as the introduction of free education and offering financial assistance in case of need;

Make higher education accessible to all on the basis of capacity by every appropriate means;

Make educational and vocational information and guidance available and accessible to all children;

Take measures to encourage regular attendance at schools and the reduction of drop-out rates.

States Parties shall take all appropriate measures to ensure that school discipline is administered in a manner consistent with the child's human dignity and in conformity with the present Convention.

States Parties shall promote and encourage international cooperation in matters relating to education, in particular with a view to contributing to the elimination of ignorance and illiteracy throughout the world and facilitating access to scientific and technical knowledge and modern teaching methods. In this regard, particular account shall be taken of the needs of developing countries.

Article 29

States Parties agree that the education of the child shall be directed to:

The development of the child's personality, talents and mental and physical abilities to their fullest potential;

The development of respect for human rights and fundamental freedoms, and for the principles enshrined in the Charter of the United Nations;

The development of respect for the child's parents, his or her own cultural identity, language and values, for the national values of the country in which the child is living, the country from which he or she may originate, and for civilizations different from his or her own;

The preparation of the child for responsible life in a free society, in the spirit of understanding, peace, tolerance, equality of sexes, and friendship among all peoples, ethnic, national, and religious groups and persons of indigenous origin;

The development of respect for the natural environment.

No part of the present article or article 28 shall be construed so as to interfere with the liberty of individuals and bodies to establish and direct educational institutions, subject always to the observance of the principle set forth in paragraph 1 of the present article and to the requirements that the education given in such institutions shall conform to such minimum standards as may be laid down by the State.

Article 30

In those States in which ethnic, religious, or linguistic minorities or persons of indigenous origin exist, a child belonging to such a minority or who is indigenous shall not be denied the right, in community with other members of his or her group, to enjoy his or her own culture, to profess and practice his or her own religion, or to use his or her own language.

Article 31

States Parties recognize the right of the child to rest and leisure, to engage in play and recreational activities appropriate to the age of the child and to participate freely in cultural life and the arts.

States Parties shall respect and promote the right of the child to participate fully in cultural and artistic life and shall encourage the provision of appropriate and equal opportunities for cultural, artistic, recreational, and leisure activity.

Article 32

States Parties recognize the right of the child to be protected from economic exploitation and from performing any work that is likely to be hazardous or to interfere with the child's education, or to be harmful to the child's health or physical, mental, spiritual, moral, or social development.

States Parties shall take legislative, administrative, social, and educational measures to ensure the implementation of the present article. To this end and having regard to the relevant provisions of other international instruments, States Parties shall in particular:

Provide for a minimum age or minimum ages for admission to employment;

Provide for appropriate regulation of the hours and conditions of employment;

Provide for appropriate penalties or other sanctions to ensure the effective enforcement of the present article.

Article 33

States Parties shall take all appropriate measures, including legislative, administrative, social, and educational measures, to protect children from the illicit use of narcotic drugs and psychotropic substances as defined in the relevant international treaties and to prevent the use of children in the illicit production and trafficking of such substances.

Article 34

States Parties undertake to protect the child from all forms of sexual exploitation and sexual abuse. For these purposes, States Parties shall in particular take all appropriate national, bilateral, and multilateral measures to prevent:

The inducement or coercion of a child to engage in any unlawful sexual activity;

The exploitative use of children in prostitution or other unlawful sexual practices;

The exploitative use of children in pornographic performances and materials.

Article 35

States Parties shall take all appropriate national, bilateral, and multilateral measures to prevent the abduction of, the sale of or traffic in children for any purpose or in any form.

Article 36

States Parties shall protect the child against all other forms of exploitation prejudicial to any aspects of the child's welfare.

Article 37

States Parties shall ensure that:

No child shall be subjected to torture or other cruel, inhuman or degrading treatment or punishment. Neither capital punishment nor life imprisonment without possibility of release shall be imposed for offenses committed by persons below eighteen years of age;

No child shall be deprived of his or her liberty unlawfully or arbitrarily. The arrest, detention, or imprisonment of a child shall be in conformity with the law and shall be used only as a measure of last resort and for the shortest appropriate period of time;

Every child deprived of liberty shall be treated with humanity and respect for the inherent dignity of the human person and in a manner which takes into account the needs of persons of his or her age. In particular, every child deprived of liberty shall be separated from adults unless it is considered in the child's best interest not to do so and shall have the right to maintain contact with his or her family through correspondence and visits, save in exceptional circumstances;

Every child deprived of his or her liberty shall have the right to prompt access to legal and other appropriate assistance, as well as the right to challenge the legality of the deprivation of his or her liberty before a court or other competent, independent and impartial authority and to a prompt decision on any such action.

Article 38

States Parties undertake to respect and to ensure respect for rules of international humanitarian law applicable to them in armed conflicts which are relevant to the child.

States Parties shall take all feasible measures to ensure that persons who have not attained the age of fifteen years do not take a direct part in hostilities.

States Parties shall refrain from recruiting any person who has not attained the age of fifteen years into their armed forces. In recruiting among those persons who have attained the age of fifteen years but who have not attained the age of eighteen years, States Parties shall endeavor to give priority to those who are oldest.

In accordance with their obligations under international humanitarian law to protect the civilian population in armed conflicts, States Parties shall take all feasible measures to ensure protection and care of children who are affected by an armed conflict.

Article 39

States Parties shall take all appropriate measures to promote physical and psychological recovery and social reintegration of a child victim of: any form of neglect, exploitation, or abuse; torture or any other form of cruel, inhuman, or degrading treatment or punishment; or armed conflicts. Such recovery and reintegration shall take place in an environment which fosters the health, self-respect, and dignity of the child.

Article 40

States Parties recognize the right of every child alleged as, accused of, or recognized as having infringed the penal law to be treated in a manner consistent with the promotion of the child's sense of dignity and worth, which reinforces the child's respect for the human rights and fundamental freedoms of others and which takes into account the child's age and the desirability of promoting the child's reintegration and the child's assuming a constructive role in society.

To this end and having regard to the relevant provisions of international instruments, States Parties shall, in particular, ensure that:

No child shall be alleged as, be accused of, or recognized as having infringed the penal law by reason of acts or omissions that were not prohibited by national or international law at the time they were committed;

Every child alleged as or accused of having infringed the penal law has at least the following guarantees:

To be presumed innocent until proven guilty according to law;

To be informed promptly and directly of the charges against him or her, and, if appropriate, through his or her parents or legal guardians and to have legal or other appropriate assistance in the preparation and presentation of his or her defense;

To have the matter determined without delay by a competent, independent and impartial authority or judicial body in a fair hearing according to law, in the presence of legal or other appropriate assistance and, unless it is considered not to be in the best interest of the child, in particular, taking into account his or her age or situation, his or her parents or legal guardians;

Not to be compelled to give testimony or to confess guilt; to examine or have examined adverse witnesses and to obtain the participation and examination of witnesses on his or her behalf under conditions of equality;

If considered to have infringed the penal law, to have this decision and any measures imposed in consequence thereof reviewed by a higher competent, independent, and impartial authority or judicial body according to law;

To have the free assistance of an interpreter if the child cannot understand or speak the language used;

To have his or her privacy fully respected at all stages of the proceedings.

States Parties shall seek to promote the establishment of laws, procedures, authorities, and institutions specifically applicable to children alleged as, accused of, or recognized as having infringed the penal law, and, in particular:

The establishment of a minimum age below which children shall be presumed not to have the capacity to infringe the penal law;

Whenever appropriate and desirable, measures for dealing with such children without resorting to judicial proceedings, providing that human rights and legal safeguards are fully respected.

A variety of dispositions, such as care, guidance, and supervision orders; counseling; probation; foster care; education and vocational training programs and other alternatives to institutional care shall be available to ensure that children are dealt with in a manner appropriate to their well-being and proportionate both to their circumstances and the offense.

Article 41

Nothing in the present Convention shall affect any provisions which are more conducive to the realization of the rights of the child and which may be contained in:

The law of a State party; or International law in force for that State.

Article 42

States Parties undertake to make the principles and provisions of the Convention widely known, by appropriate and active means, to adults and children alike.

Article 43

For the purpose of examining the progress made by States Parties in achieving the realization of the obligations undertaken in the present Convention, there shall be established a Committee on the Rights of the Child, which shall carry out the functions hereinafter provided.

The Committee shall consist of ten experts of high moral standing and recognized competence in the field covered by this Convention. The members of the Committee shall be elected by States Parties from among their nationals and shall serve in their personal capacity, consideration being given to equitable geographical distribution, as well as to the principal legal systems.

The members of the Committee shall be elected by secret ballot from a list of persons nominated by States Parties. Each State Party may nominate one person from among its own nationals.

The initial election to the Committee shall be held no later than six months after the date of the entry into force of the present Convention and thereafter every second year. At least four months before the date of each election, the Secretary-General of the United Nations shall address a letter to States Parties inviting them to submit their nominations within two months. The Secretary-General shall subsequently prepare a list in alphabetical order of all persons thus nominated, indicating States Parties which have nominated them and shall submit it to the States Parties to the present Convention.

The elections shall be held at meetings of States Parties convened by the Secretary-General at United Nations Headquarters. At those meetings, for which two-thirds of States Parties shall constitute a quorum, the persons elected to the Committee shall be those who obtain the largest number of votes and an absolute majority of the votes of the representatives of States Parties present and voting.

The members of the Committee shall be elected for a term of four years. They shall be eligible for reelection if renominated. The term of five of the members elected at the first election shall expire at the end of two years; immediately after the first election, the names of these five members shall be chosen by lot by the Chairman of the meeting.

If a member of the Committee dies or resigns or declares that for any other cause he or she can no longer perform the duties of the Committee, the State Party which nominated the member shall appoint another expert from among its nationals to serve for the remainder of the term, subject to the approval of the Committee.

The Committee shall establish its own rules of procedure.

The Committee shall elect its officers for a period of two years.

The meetings of the Committee shall normally be held at United Nations Headquarters or at any other convenient place as determined by the Committee. The Committee shall normally meet annually. The duration of the meetings of the Committee shall be determined and reviewed, if necessary, by a meeting of the States Parties to the present Convention, subject to the approval of the General Assembly.

The Secretary-General of the United Nations shall provide the necessary staff and facilities for the effective performance of the functions of the Committee under the present Convention.

With the approval of the General Assembly, the members of the Committee established under the present Convention shall receive emoluments from United Nations resources on such terms and conditions as the Assembly may decide.

Article 44

States Parties undertake to submit to the Committee, through the Secretary-General of the United Nations, reports on the measures they have adopted which give effect to the rights recognized herein and on the progress made on the enjoyment of those rights:

Within two years of the entry into force of the Convention for the State Party concerned;

Thereafter every five years.

Reports made under the present article shall indicate factors and difficulties, if any, affecting the degree of fulfillment of the obligations under the present Convention. Reports shall also contain sufficient information to provide the Committee with a comprehensive understanding of the implementation of the Convention in the country concerned.

A State Party which has submitted a comprehensive initial report to the Committee need not, in its subsequent reports submitted in accordance with paragraph 1 (b) of the present article, repeat basic information previously provided.

The Committee may request from States Parties further information relevant to the implementation of the Convention.

The Committee shall submit to the General Assembly, through the Economic and Social Council, every two years, reports on its activities.

States Parties shall make their reports widely available to the public in their own countries.

Article 45

In order to foster the effective implementation of the Convention and to encourage international cooperation in the field covered by the Convention:

The specialized agencies, the United Nations Children's Fund and other United Nations organs shall be entitled to be represented at the consideration of the implementation of such provisions of the present Convention as fall within the scope of their mandate. The Committee may invite the specialized agencies, the United Nations Children's Fund and other competent bodies as it may consider appropriate to provide expert advice on the implementation of the Convention in areas falling within the scope of their respective mandates. The Committee may invite the specialized agencies, the United Nations Children's Fund and other United Nations organs to submit reports on the implementation of the Convention in areas falling within the scope of their activities;

The Committee shall transmit, as it may consider appropriate, to the specialized agencies, the United Nations Children's Fund and other competent bodies, any reports from States Parties that contain a request, or indicate a need, for technical advice or assistance, along with the Committee's observations and suggestions, if any, on these requests or indications;

The Committee may recommend to the General Assembly to request the Secretary-General to undertake on its behalf studies on specific issues relating to the rights of the child;

The Committee may make suggestions and general recommendations based on information received pursuant to articles 44 and 45 of the present Convention. Such suggestions and general recommendations shall be transmitted to any State Party concerned and reported to the General Assembly, together with comments, if any, from States Parties.

Article 46

The present Convention shall be open for signature by all States.

Article 47

The present Convention is subject to ratification. Instruments of ratification shall be deposited with the Secretary-General of the United Nations.

Article 48

The present Convention shall remain open for accession by any State. The instruments of accession shall be deposited with the Secretary-General of the United Nations.

Article 49

The present Convention shall enter into force on the thirtieth day following the date of deposit with the Secretary-General of the United Nations of the twentieth instrument of ratification or accession.

For each State ratifying or acceding to the Convention after the deposit of the twentieth instrument of ratification or accession, the Convention shall enter into force on the thirtieth day after the deposit by such State of its instrument of ratification or accession.

Article 50

Any State Party may propose an amendment and file it with the Secretary-General of the United Nations. The Secretary-General shall thereupon communicate the proposed amendment to States Parties, with a request that they indicate whether they favor a conference of States Parties for the purpose of considering and voting upon the proposals. In the event that, within four months from the date of such communication, at least one-third of the States Parties favor such a conference, the Secretary-General shall convene the conference under the auspices of the United Nations. Any amendment adopted by a majority of States Parties present and voting at the conference shall be submitted to the General Assembly for approval.

An amendment adopted in accordance with paragraph 1 of the present article shall enter into force when it has been approved by the General Assembly of the United Nations and accepted by a two-thirds majority of States Parties.

When an amendment enters into force, it shall be binding on those States Parties which have accepted it, other States Parties still being bound by the provisions of the present Convention and any earlier amendments which they have accepted.

Article 51

The Secretary-General of the United Nations shall receive and circulate to all States the text of reservations made by States at the time of ratification or accession.

A reservation incompatible with the object and purpose of the present Convention shall not be permitted.

Reservations may be withdrawn at any time by notification to that effect addressed to the Secretary-General of the United Nations, who shall then inform all States. Such notification shall take effect on the date on which it is received by the Secretary-General.

Article 52

A State Party may denounce the present Convention by written notification to the Secretary-General of the United Nations. Denunciation becomes effective one year after the date of receipt of the notification by the Secretary-General.

Article 53

The Secretary-General of the United Nations is designated as the depositary of the present Convention.

Article 54

The original of the present Convention, of which the Arabic, Chinese, English, French, Russian, and Spanish texts are equally authentic, shall be deposited with the Secretary-General of the United Nations.

In witness thereof the undersigned plenipotentiaries, being duly authorized thereto by their respective governments, have signed the present Convention.